CHOOSE YOUR PLACE

RETHINKING HOME AS YOU AGE

AMANDA LAMBERT AND
LESLIE ECKFORD

The information provided in this book is designed to provide helpful information on the subjects discussed. References are provided for informational purposes only and do not constitute endorsements of any websites, companies, products, organizations or programs. Readers should be aware that the websites listed in this book may change.

ISBN: 978-0-578-76863-2 (paperback)

CONTENTS

ACKNOWLEDGMENTS

When we set out to write this book, we agreed "let's fill it with sto-ries." We have been most fortunate to find many wonderful people who have not only shared their stories but also their kindness and generous spirit. We are grateful. For privacy, we have changed the names, locations and identifying details of most of the people described. In addition, we extend our thanks to Susan Dickenson for the inspiring account of her amazing dad, Richard Jorgensen; and to Ryan Murphy for introducing us to people who know the real upsides to downsizing. We have truly enjoyed getting to know all the different individuals in this book who share a talent for finding solutions.

And, our gratitude, always, to our trusted editor, Lisa Goldstein Kieda.

INTRODUCTION

"Today is the first day of the rest of your life." Though this cliché from the 60's was overused, there's a reason it appeared everywhere. This early self-help mantra is a powerful reminder to choose the direction of your life. It insists that you take stock now and create your unique path. You can envision your future and take steps today to make it happen. We invite you to come along with us in this book on a new adventure. And, it all begins with home.

Maybe you're thinking, "I don't have time for an adventure right now." Chances are, you are still working and busy with everyday life. You've reached some milestones. You had promotions, and could be training the next generation for the position you started in. You might be an empty nester, and are watching your parents grow old. Retirement is a siren song that may beckon you. Or, frankly, leaving your work world doesn't interest you, for now. You may not have done much planning yet. You know that you want it to be different than what your parents' generation had. But how?

For us, the critical question is "Where do you want to live?" Most of us, of any age, know where we DON'T want to live in old age: the dreaded nursing home. Unfortunately, some of us, at some point, may not have a choice about living in that setting. Chronic health conditions and physical decline may simply need it. Yet, there is a lot of life to be lived before that possibility. Where do you want to be and what do you want to be doing with your life until then?

We know that change is in the air. Many aging adults are flat out rejecting the corporate senior living model...at least for as long as they can. Remember the famous scene from the movie Network? Picture older adults opening their windows and yelling "We're mad as hell and we're not going to take it anymore!" People who have lived their lives by their own choices want to continue to have control. While writing this book, we have met older adults deciding for themselves where they want to live in their old age. We have encountered some fascinating ideas and some brave souls. We have hunted far and wide to bring you the stories of their decisions about how and where and with whom to live.

When will you make these choices? Will you wait until a health crisis forces you to move? Will you wait until your children or doctor insist that your present home does not meet your needs or is unsafe?

If you are in your fifties or early sixties, we are glad that you have found this book. Now is the time, people! Join us as we explore the homes in this book that others have chosen. Let us introduce you to the people who have thought out what they want and how they want to live in this next chapter.

A WORD ABOUT COVID-19

As we are finishing this book in the summer of 2020, we are easily distracted by thoughts of the coronavirus. Constant bad news, concerns about health and safety of elderly loved ones, the changing landscape of potential treatments and vaccines and of course, the tragic loss of life in the US and around the globe.

In many respects, our book comes at a time when everyone, no matter what age, is reminded of how brief life can be. If we have all learned one thing, it is how quickly a crisis can turn life upside down. Outside forces can completely interrupt personal goals. Our boring routines of "normal life" are suddenly longed for.

We think that this book may be just right for the post-COVID-19 world. A theme that you will find throughout this book is "think about it differently." We want you to know that choices about aging and housing are out there for you to consider. Planning is important, but so is flexibility.

As authors, we have no way of predicting exactly how senior housing markets will adjust to life after the virus. There were already efforts to improve group care, but this pandemic will require a whole new vision. Certainly there will be changes. We think that there could be some positive outcomes. Clearly, many developments for seniors and multigenerational living will have to be re-designed to prevent contagion. At the same time, they can be modified to enhance quality of life.

We will address post-COVID thoughts and ideas when relevant in chapters. We will have these in a separate heading. If we can re-con-nect with people we have interviewed, we will include their thoughts about how the virus has affected their choices as well.

Please use this book as a guide to taking a proactive approach to where you want to live as you age. To use a well-worn phrase, "think outside of the box." Some of the best possibilities are still out there awaiting you.

I

NECESSITY IS THE MOTHER OF INVENTION

INTRODUCTION

Take a deep breath. Aging is upon us. Where will we live? Who will we live with? Who will help us when we need care? How will we pay for it? These are questions that many of us and our families are pondering.

There are so many new and creative notions about senior housing that they don't all have names! Housing options are only limited by people's imaginations. Some groups of aging people have already formed their own living situation. Others are coming up with new and innovative ways to share costs and build community.

Not everyone wants or needs the typical assisted living. Certainly not everyone can afford it. The average cost of assisted living in the US is $3,700 per month[1] and that cost rises as more care is needed.

In our previous books, we have consistently promoted and supported the choice to age at home. We believe that being in one's own familiar home and living with as much independence as possible is the ideal aging situation. Over the years, however, we have learned that "home" may be in many different places. Home could be one's long-term home. It may be a smaller, downsized, more accessible house or condo or apartment. It may be a home in some version of senior housing. It may be a suite or apartment attached to a younger family member's home. Or, it could be a boarding house-style home with non-relatives sharing common areas. In any scenario, we find that the person's inclusion in the process of choosing their home is essential to their sense of well-being.

In this book, we will explore as many different options that combine the notions of "aging" and "home" as we can find. We think that you will enjoy learning about many new ideas and configurations of a household. Clearly, with so many of us entering our third act, demand is high. Many do not have the savings that their parents had. Necessity drives us to be creative and more flexible in deciding what home will be.

WE'VE BEEN WATCHING AND TAKING NOTES

As baby boomers, we've had a front row seat watching our parents navigate the uncharted waters of increased life span. Much like pioneers, our parents have been the first to live in a bubble of time when medical advances have added years to life expectancy. At the same time, quality of life and health during old age still generally diminishes. In spite of our best health building efforts, some parts of aging are unavoidable.

Sometimes, it appears that luck has more to do with it. We have seen individuals who appeared to have the healthiest lifestyles get felled by a stroke. And, it seems everyone knows a die-hard smoker who lives to 97. It can be a crapshoot. Many will still face a longer life hobbled with illness and greater dependency. In spite of scientific advancements, aging continues to be a phase of life that includes decline in physical and mental abilities. Chronic illnesses and conditions are more likely. The immune system weakens as one grows older and it is harder to fend off disease.

We have seen our parents accept the hard realities of needing assistance. In many cases, a health crisis can lead to an untimely move. We have been there with them to say goodbye to what they thought were forever homes. Those homes are like a member of the family. We have felt the pain and loss alongside our parents. Their choices of where to live seemed more finite in the past and leading in one direction: the old folks home. As Betty Friedan confirms in The Fountain of Age[2], many of us see the nursing home as a death sentence.

Still, those who are aging are very motivated to do whatever they can to have the best possible outcome. We want control of our life and our health. The anti-aging and fitness industries are a gold mine. We spend every free minute exercising and taking supplements and eliminating unhealthy habits. Some of us will reach that sweet spot of physical and mental health and vigor and extra years. Even with that happy forecast, we may not have the energy or money to maintain the large family-sized homes we have been in for decades.

Unlike how it may have been for our younger selves, it becomes harder and less appealing to literally move on from one setting to another. The stakes are higher if one makes a poor decision about housing. Financially, most older people can't keep the options open to double back if things don't work out in the new place. We have known some who can. They are urged by their adult children to move from the large family home to a smaller home, such as an apartment or condo. They may agree, on the condition that the house doesn't go on the market until a trial period at the new place works out. We've even seen some people sell the old house, find the new smaller home miserable and buy back the old house.

Some older adults have moved across the country or across the state to be closer to grown children and grandchildren. Or the opposite. One person we know grieved heavily when her husband of many decades died following a long, painful illness. After many months, she emerged with a new idea and new direction for her future. She realized that she longed to return to her free-wheeling, hippie roots in California. She gave away or sold all of her household belongings and put the house in New England on the market. Significantly lighter, she packed up a few bags, kissed her children and grandchildren goodbye, and headed across the country.

Not long after arriving and settling in, she realized how dismayed she was by the changes in California since her youth. She had remembered a charming small town. It hardly had anything in common with her earlier memories. She missed her family, her friends and her crafts circle back east. Her daughter came and they made the road trip back to her "real home" together. She wouldn't be able to afford to buy back the house where she had raised her family. She would find an apartment and make it work. She noted the silver lining: at least she had the downsizing done.

LEARNING FROM EXPERIENCE

The "newly aging" have the experience of seeing what did and did not work for their parents' generation. We have seen our parents age in place, move to assisted living or skilled nursing and expect to improve on that. But how?

There are already significant trends that are different from the previous generation. Here are a few that we have observed:

- Downsizing has become a mantra for agers in the know. They have seen how detrimental excessive material possessions can be. They may have been the ones left with the responsibility of unloading a houseful of unwanted possessions for their parents.[3] They know how emotionally draining, time consuming and expensive this undertaking can be. They want to purge the things that are no longer useful in their own lives and the sooner the better.

- The thrill of home ownership is losing its luster. The largest growth in numbers of renters are now people over the age of 60.[4] Home ownership is grand when you have the motivation and the constitution to mow the lawn and repair the leaky sink. Now, people are choosing to hand those responsibilities to the landlord.

- Next Avenue reported that US government data reveals concerning financial trends for those over 65. The article states "A financial asset ownership gap among boomers has been growing. The National Institute on Retirement Security report indicated that from 2004 to 2016, the share of financial assets owned by the wealthiest 5% of boomer households grew from 52% in 2004 to 60% in 2016. And the share owned by the top 10% rose from 68% to 75%."[5] Meanwhile the shares of monetary assets owned by the bottom 50% of boomers shrank from 3% to under 2%. What does this mean? The gap widens between the haves and have nots as people age. Economic hardship is growing. The article further states that housing inequality for boomers is a significant problem and likely to get worse. This sets the stage for alternative affordable options for housing.

- Older adults recognize the dangers of social isolation and want an alternative that is not institutional. They want a personal experience that they can control and cost is a factor too! We have witnessed an unprecedented expansion of the senior living and care industry for our parents' generation. For many this is now an unappealing prospect. The cookie-cutter, one size fits all surroundings are a turn off.

THE MOST INTRIGUING OPTIONS FOR SENIOR LIVING

We dove into the project of this book with eyes wide open. We believe that we have found some of the more practical living solutions for people as they age. Some will sound very familiar, but with refined polish for seniors. Some are brand new ideas. We introduce them here and go into much more detail in later chapters of the book:

- The Allure of Cohousing – A concept borrowed from Europe, cohousing communities have developed in many different configurations around the US. We will provide definitions and meet some people who are over 60 who are living this lifestyle.
- The Golden Girls Inspired Home – Home sharing is not new, but the emphasis on elder residents is. We will introduce some people who are doing this with great success and give ideas on how to start on this path.
- The Family Tradition-Moving in with the Kids – This multigenerational family option has definitely been around for millennia, and had only recently fallen out of favor in modern American life after World War II. For some families, it never really went away. For others, they are trying it for the first time. We will meet families who are making this work.
- New Frontiers in Senior Housing – Slowly, developers are getting the message. The boomers do not want to be shunted

away from the action in cookie cutter senior housing. They
want more individuality and style and connectivity to other
generations. We find some great examples to show you.

- Becoming an Expat – What is it really like in this day and age
to leave the US for a more senior focused culture? Is it really
less expensive? We ask people who have done it.

WHY EACH OF US NEEDS A PLAN...AND A PLAN B

As you read this book, you will meet many aging individuals who
have faced these challenges before us. Some have done very well. You
will hear from their stories that no matter where they have lived, they
have made their choice a priority. Their sense of self and their involvement in the choice of place has been a prime concern. That is
the standard of success that we have looked for. We think that is because they have made a plan in advance and communicated that plan
to family, either directly or by advance directive.

We've observed that some people have embraced the notion that
life is all about change. There may be unpredictable events. Instead
of throwing up their hands to let the fates take them where they may,
they stay open to adjusting the plan. There must be a contingency
plan. These "super planners," if you will, recognize that financial
support can easily disappear. This may require a change in address. It
may mean that relocating to another state to be closer to family is going to make more sense. From this perspective, refusing to hear more
options can be counter-productive.

For others, who do not have a plan, there can be a less than opti-
mal outcome. Any one of us may have a stroke or develop an illness
that makes it difficult for us to speak for ourselves. This can be temporary or this can be permanent. Clearly, this leaves a person very vul-
nerable. When there is no stated plan for this scenario, even the most
well-intentioned family will have to guess where that person would
prefer to be. People without a plan, for all intents and purposes, have
given their deciding vote to someone else. In the best case scenario, it
all works out for the best. But, in other cases, it can produce a feeling
of disconnection with oneself and one's dignity.

In the course of our research for this book, we have met some incredible people who have really thought this through. Some families call it their "Master Plan." Some may refer to it as "Plan Z." They have left a "road map," a "strategy," or a "guide." Whatever they call it, they stress the following:

- Communication – A family needs to gather around the table or a conference call to discuss the plan. Questions must be allowed. Finances MUST be transparent. The communication is an open channel, not a one time only conversation.
- Flexibility – We noticed that a spirit of "let's try this and see" signaled an openness to new possibilities that may work just fine, for at least a time.
- Sharing the Reins – Recognizing that there may come a time when you cannot make every decision for yourself is hard. The fears and concerns about that can be reduced if you know in advance who will represent you. You can have the hard, heart-to-heart talks with a person (family or otherwise) who you appoint as your agent so that they can honor your priorities.

Usually, discussions about advance planning focus on medical outcomes. However, we have come to understand that where one lives needs forethought. We think that this "home-inclusive" advance planning is so important that we will have a later chapter devoted to it. We will select some people who are coming to terms with their own aging. We will do some organizing with them using Amanda's unique approach that she has refined in her geriatric care practice. We will share their stories with you as they consider what home means to them.

2

THE ALLURE OF COHOUSING

WHAT EXACTLY IS COHOUSING?

Cohousing is hot! The idea originated in Denmark, but you will see why this concept is gaining steam and attracting people of all ages in this country. The definition of cohousing is a community where people own their individual homes plus a share of common areas. Common areas can include outdoor space and a clubhouse with kitchen, living and dining rooms. The community is an intentional community of private homes clustered around these shared spaces. Residents prepare and share meals several times a week. Cohousing can be a group of separate homes, condominiums, or even one home where several people share space.

Originally, cohousing communities were intended for families who wanted to be closer to each other. People wanted to raise their children together, which meant the neighborhoods were multigenerational.

Some cohousing communities are for seniors only. There are approximately 168 cohousing communities in the United States. This includes 14 that are senior focused.[6] Development plans are underway for another 140. Most cohousing communities have the following in common:

- They are structured like a condominium with a homeowners association, but are self-managed.

- Owners make collective decisions, usually by consensus. Some cohousing communities use a decision making process called Dynamic Governance.[7] Dynamic Governance uses the governing principle of consent as the basis for decision-making. Unlike consensus, the focus is not on agreement. It is a process by which each member is able to explain their reasoned objection to a proposal. The group then problem-solves to find a solution to the objection. This system allows for a relatively quick decision-making process while at the same time bringing in the wisdom of the group.
- Committees oversee the financial, administrative and maintenance work. This eliminates the need for a management company.
- Each owner is expected and sometimes required to pitch in with cooking, cleaning, and fixing minor problems.
- Costs can sometimes be significant to buy in. Yet, according to the Cohousing Association of America, pricing is comparable to housing in the area. There may also be monthly homeowners fees.

You can find an entire description of co-housing options at www. cohousing.org. With vast numbers of baby boomers reaching retirement age, cohousing can be an attractive option. It offers the best of both worlds: community and privacy.

A COHOUSING MEMBER TELLS US WHAT IT'S LIKE

"My husband puts it this way: living in cohousing gives us a basic level of support at this age that we wouldn't have in our own single family home. That support lowers the baseline anxiety of living for us. There's more of a safety net." Marianne, age 65.

Marianne, her husband and teenage daughter moved into an established cohousing community in the northwest about 15 years ago. At the time, their oldest child had moved out on her own and they realized that they were ready for a change. They had always been interested in cohousing and had good friends who lived in such a place nearby. They were familiar with sharing space. In fact, in their single family house, they had rented to housemates to live with their family. They did a lot of research about cohousing. Even so, Marianne found that there was much to learn about the experience that could only happen when living it. "You really won't know what it's like until you do it." For her, the organization of group meetings and committees made a lot of sense.

Marianne finds that the consensus process in her cohousing neighborhood is effective, but a lot of work. She gave the example of a recent project to add solar panels to the buildings. Because residents own their own homes there, but have some shared rooftops, much detail, including costs and how people would pay, had to be worked out. She thinks that because the members of the resident group were already dedicated to make the consensus process work, it was less contentious.

Marianne describes numerous advantages for her to live in cohousing. She likes to feel connected to the people around her. She strives to live with intention. She benefits from the collective wisdom of her neighbors. And she is motivated to put consensus decision making into practice.

If she could change anything about her neighborhood, it would be to have a greater commitment from the other residents. There are about 50 adults there. She sees that some are much less involved and are "kind of zoned out." She would prefer that more of them would contribute more and consider the "depth of their intentions."

Marianne lives in a multigenerational cohousing community which includes families with children and aging members. Some homeowners do not have local extended family and thus their cohousing neighbors fill in those roles to some extent. It was not designed for aging per se. She says that a number of the founding members are aging in place there. Some members have died there. But she has also seen a neighbor who struggled with her increasing needs for assistive care. The group was willing to help out with shopping and meals, but could not provide personal care. Eventually, that occupant's family intervened and moved her to a senior residence that could. Now age 65, Marianne has not given a lot of thought to what she would do if she were in that situation. But, based on observing her neighbor's experience, she is open to moving again.

WHAT HAPPENED TO MARIANNE AND HER HUSBAND WHEN COVID HIT?

We checked back with Marianne a few months after the pandemic began.

What has it been like in your cohousing space since the onset of the pandemic?
Like everyone, we have been concerned. Fortunately we had a team of five people (RN's and health care providers) who gathered to help create safe guidelines for our community. Since we set that in place, I think we have felt more relaxed and trusting of our situation. And it's been over three months now, so we are definitely more 'used' to this than we were in the initial weeks.

How have daily activities with neighbors changed or remained the same?
We no longer have shared meals, either in the common house or in our individual homes. As far as I know, none of us go into each other's houses right now. We don't meet or do any group activities or parties or meetings in the common house. We do not allow anyone to sleep in the guest room. On the bright side, so many people are working from home, and so neighbors are around more. We chat outside on the paths at six feet, a handful of people might do an outside happy hour at six foot distance. If someone is going food shopping, they often send out an email, offering to pick things up for others. We have taken our community meetings, which used to be about once a month, onto Zoom. We meet for a shorter time but more frequently. Currently we share joys and concerns twice a month, and have business meetings twice a month. The kids were initially inside or outside only with their parents for the first month or two. Now, they have learned social distancing and ways to 'play outside' together safely.

Have you felt more or less isolated than before sheltering in place?
We were lucky to see each other on the paths, outside and on Zoom meetings. So, not so much isolated from this community. But we all

would like to share meals, have events, give hugs, and see our friends and family in the wider community...

Do you feel confident that where you live is safe and secure?
We are doing pretty well. We have a crew that sanitizes surfaces in common spaces daily. We mostly agree upon principles of social distancing, hand washing, not touching your face.

Do you wish that you lived somewhere else?
No, unless it would be some vacation home in a gorgeous place where I was quarantined with my husband and adult kids and some friends. But that's wishful thinking. We are extremely lucky living here, in community. Many people step outside at lunch time to socialize with neighbors. Lots of flower and vegetable gardening is happening. The garden vegetables help me stretch out my food shopping so I don't have to go more than once every two to three weeks, since I have access to fresh lettuce, greens, etc every day! Fingers crossed, but none of us has gotten sick with the virus yet. One of our members sewed a ton of face masks for people here. Many of us designed prayer flags and they are hanging with our good wishes in our central area.

A FEW EXAMPLES OF URBAN COHOUSING COMMUNITIES

Some cannot imagine living without the hustle and bustle of city surroundings. Below are some examples of urban co-housing communities with descriptions taken directly from their websites. These communities have ready access to city life.

Swan's Market Cohousing in Oakland, California
"Swan's is a 20 unit cohousing community located in the preserved and retrofitted 1917 Swan's Market building in the historic Old Oakland neighborhood. Swan's has all age groups from infants to seniors.

This urban setting is walkable and accessible to public transportation. Several shops, stores and restaurants are nearby.

Community amenities include a 3,500 square foot common house with large kitchen and dining area. There is a kids' playroom, exercise room, laundry, workshop, community garden, guest room, large patio for dining/entertaining."

Puget Ridge Cohousing in Seattle, Washington
"About fifty people, one-quarter of whom are children, live at Puget Ridge, in twenty-three duplex and triplex units that face one another in a village-like setting. The community members range in age from two to eighty-six years old and people work in a variety of ways in and out of the home.

The 4,000 square-foot common house is central to the community's life. It provides a shared "third place" — a place to run into and visit with neighbors, share meals, have meetings, celebrate with private or community events, pick up mail, and more.

The property is landscaped with native species and includes fruit trees. There is a dedicated organic garden, including a hoop house, where residents grow vegetables, flowers, and berries. The garden is maintained by regular work parties and its bounty is available to all residents, including use in community meals."

Cambridge Cohousing in Cambridge, Massachusetts
"Cambridge Cohousing opened in the winter of 1998. It has 41 units from townhouses to studio apartments and a large common house with many amenities. It also has several unique green spaces unusual for an urban development. The community has diverse age groups."

Takoma Village Cohousing in Washington DC
"Takoma Village is a multi-generational cohousing community made up of 43 privately owned townhouses and flats. The community usually includes 65 to 70 adults and 15 to 20 children. Residents range in age from infants to octogenarians. Members come from many ethnic, religious, and cultural traditions. There are residents of differing sexual orientations, and neighbors with varying levels of ability. They are a mix of omnivores, vegetarians, and vegans who nevertheless enjoy sharing meals together.

The homes at Takoma Village are a mix of 20 flats and 23 townhouses. Nearly 90 percent of the homes are visitable by people in wheelchairs."

EXAMPLES OF RURAL COHOUSING COMMUNITIES

In contrast to urban cohousing communities, we have listed some examples of rural settings. The descriptions of these communities are taken from their websites. You may notice that many of these have significant acreage, yet are accessible to urban areas.

Heartwood Cohousing in Bayfield, Colorado
"Heartwood near Durango, Colorado is located on 361 acres of pine forest, meadows, and pastureland. Heartwood is a rural cohousing community made up of people of all ages and from all walks of life. There are 24 homes that represent a diversity of ages and family units. Some of the members have been here since the beginning of Heartwood and some have arrived in the 20 years since then."

Nubanusit Neighborhood and Farm in Peterborough, New Hampshire
"Nubanusit condo is green and environmentally designed, quality built, and super energy-efficient. The homes cluster along pedestrian pathways adjacent to our farm fields and the Nubanusit Brook.

The community shares 113 acres of farmland, fields and woodlands with trails, a pond, and nearly a mile of riverfront. They are contracted with a farmer who operates a CSA (Community Supported Agriculture) farm. The age range of residents is from 1 year to over 80 years."

NANCY'S COHOUSING EXPERIENCE

"I decided to do it because of the people."
About 25 years ago, Nancy had been friends with a group of people who were creating their own cohousing community in an urban area outside of Seattle. She had observed the long and complex process that they had been through. They had to find the right piece of land. The group worked with an architect to design a community that would include large, multilevel homes and small single floor units. They planned community buildings for socializing, meetings and dining. All combined with an inviting outdoor environment that allowed for gardening and connecting paths for walkability.

It took a great deal of energy and years to finally get construction underway.

So, when one family in the group who had a three bedroom house under construction had to pull out at the last minute (to move to another state to care for an elder family member), Nancy knew that this was an opportunity for her. She was a single mother of teenagers. Her kids were friends of some of the other kids about to move into the cohousing community. It seemed like it would be a win-win for all of her family.

She just needed to see how the group worked together. She was invited to come to a consensus meeting before finalizing the house purchase. "I got a chance to see them in action." What impressed her was that though there were natural leaders in the group, "they were not trying to set forth their own agenda." Instead, Nancy says that she was able to see "the way the meeting was handled...with respect and with dedication to consensus." That was a turning point, and the process she witnessed cinched the deal for her.

Once she joined the group officially, she grew "pretty darned excited about what we were about to do." She worked with her soon to be neighbors to set paving stones for the walkways. At the time, she was 49 years old. "I was in good shape and I'm glad, because it takes a lot of labor to create cohousing." After moving in, Nancy saw some changes for her family. She says that while it is a multigenerational community, for her teenagers, it was a little too "adult-centric." It was not easy for them to get transportation to activities outside of their home as bus lines were not so accessible as when they lived closer to the city. Consequently, one of her children decided to move in with their father and the other soon moved out on her own. She understands that, for them, it wasn't the fit that it was for her.

Now, Nancy is 74. "I recently realized that I've lived (in cohousing) longer than anywhere else I have lived in my life." She sees many advantages to living in this community. "It's hard to work with others, but if you can be flexible with them, it can be richly rewarding." She says it is a warm environment that is safe and secure. She has found that being a part of this has encouraged her own personal growth. She has learned to "own her own stuff" and sees her neighbors do that as well. Overall, she feels acceptance from others.

She sees her community evolving. This year they have worked with an attorney to upgrade their condominium bylaws to new state standards. She is amazed at the 64-page length of the document. She hears of friends outside of her cohousing who have to deal with similar issues in condominium HOA's that are not cohousing. Nancy is grateful that her group still works with intention for consensus and without the contentious atmosphere that is often experienced in other settings.

She also has recognized in her multigenerational community that "people's lives are not necessarily synchronous in modern life." She wishes that some of the younger members had more time to give to the community.

When asked if she plans to age in place there, Nancy is a pragmatist. She is currently in good health and loves where she lives. She continues to be a participant and contributor. She has not given a lot of thought to where she would move, but she easily admits that her cohousing environment is "not set up" for aging. She does not see it as a realistic option for new elders to move into. "This community requires work. I want elders to know that."

WHAT HAPPENED TO NANCY AFTER COVID HIT?

What has it been like in your cohousing space since the onset of the pandemic? How have daily activities with neighbors changed or remained the same?
We've closed off the Common House to all activities besides distributing and retrieving mail, doing laundry, and working in the shop. It's been a huge loss to everybody, but my life hasn't been badly affected. I'm responsible for sanitizing the door handles of the Common House and other high-touch places on Fridays. Other people take different days. I miss cooking and eating together, watching movies, and having other activities – concerts, meetings, etc. We've had Zoom check-ins weekly, (an hour or so, as opposed to monthly three hour business meetings with 30-40 minutes for check ins). All told, I'd say everyone is grateful to live here. We are connected with community despite the isolation. Life is definitely constricted, though with the

advent of warmer weather we've been able to hang outside together at a distance. My neighbor has been "holding court" on her porch and I often take my breakfast or lunch out and sit close enough to chat with her. It has been stressful for families with children, with parents working from home. Nobody here is having to work in a high-exposure workplace, fortunately. We are well aware of our relative privilege.

Have you felt more or less isolated than before sheltering in place?
Have certainly been more isolated – I miss the "running around" in the larger community that I used to do. My rowing group and dance and exercise classes have been cancelled. Although there's some Zoom activity, which is sweet and helpful, it's not what I need!

Do you feel confident that where you live is safe and secure?
Yes, so far. I feel blessed to be here. None of the 60-odd residents has been affected by the illness. One family immediately moved their grandmother from her assisted living facility and into their home here in our cohousing when someone at the grandmother's assisted living facility was positive. They put a clear plastic divider down the middle of their unit, and lived next to her like that for over two weeks. Amazing! She has since moved back to the facility.

Do you wish that you lived somewhere else?
Nope!

PROS AND CONS OF COHOUSING

PROS:

1. Cohousing provides socialization and community. Unlike moving into a typical residential neighborhood or building, people move into cohousing with the intention to know and interact with their neighbors. Frequent and more meaningful interactions are a characteristic of co-housing.
2. A sense of purpose. Each person in the cohousing community has a role to play and responsibilities. The personal

connections that people have with one another fosters a caring, supportive and compassionate environment.

3. Universal Design. Starting a cohousing community from scratch allows for certain design features that can be initiated from the beginning. A few examples include no step entry, wider hallways and doorways, and grab bars. Aging in place is far easier when accessibility is not an issue later.

4. Living with a diverse group of people can be stimulating and educational.

5. Sharing expenses can have a financial benefit.

6. Environmental benefits: Many cohousing communities preserve open space. Sharing kitchen and laundry space eliminates the need for each person to have their own appliances. Transportation and shopping can be shared too.

7. Downsizing is a natural consequence of the co-housing experience. People moving from a standard single family home are choosing to live in a cohousing unit that simply has less square footage. You can do the Marie Kondo method and live only with possessions that bring you joy!

8. You still have your private space to retreat to. Although you share meals and responsibilities, you still have your privacy.

CONS:

1. If you want to live near an urban area, land can be extremely difficult to find and expensive to develop. The cost of buying or renting in a co-housing community may be prohibitively expensive for many people.

2. Conversely, if you want a rural community, medical support services can be scarce. What happens if you have an illness or accident and need extensive rehab or home health?

3. For some, cohousing is too much togetherness. It is expected that you are an active participant in the community which can require significant time... and well... togetherness.

4. Consensus sounds so good... but it can be a challenging decision making process if you aren't used to it.

5. If you are aging and widowed or single, cohousing can appear

as something that would offer you safety and security. But, it may not work if everyone in the community is looking for that from their neighbors. There needs to be some variety of strengths and skills in the group.

6. If you are thinking of designing a cohousing community with like-minded friends, start now! Several cohousing residents who had personal experience with founding a community emphasized that starting a residence from scratch involves a lot of labor and years of time to design, organize and start construction. This takes strength and endurance and so the younger you are, the better.

IS COHOUSING RIGHT FOR YOU?

THIS IS FOR YOU IF:

- If you value working together in a collaborative environment to solve issues, this could be a good fit.
- You like being a part of a sharing community. You enjoy having assigned responsibilities and tasks that benefit everyone.
- Socialization is important. Being a part of a diverse and/or multigenerational community is appealing to you. You share the values of the community that you are buying into.
- Conflict with other residents is something you feel comfortable handling.
- You feel confident in the financial commitment that is required. Costs may go up through time.

STAY CLEAR IF:

- Do you have direct experience with a neighborhood association or homeowners' association? Committee or other community meetings? What has that been like for you? If you detest hearing what the other person's point of view is, or think it is all endless discussion, cohousing may not be for you.
- Privacy is extremely important to you. Sharing meals or other

common spaces makes you uncomfortable. Although you will have your own living space, the expectation is that you will share some meals. And so will community tasks like transportation, cleaning, finances, committee work, cooking, etc.

- You don't like being told what to do and when to do it! Cohousing comes with a shared commitment to serving all members of the community.
- Your financial commitment is tenuous. Expenses can go up and if you don't have confidence in your ability to absorb costs, then cohousing may not be for you.

3

THE GOLDEN GIRLS INSPIRED HOUSE: RENTING OR BUYING, TOGETHER

Developing a true cohousing community takes significant invest-ment... and land. That's why more and more people are looking at single-family homes with room for several renters as a viable alterna-tive. Think of it as having several roommates, but with rules.

Cohousing may not be the exact term for the variety of arrange-ments that people are creating to share costs and space. Many peo-ple are referring to this configuration as homesharing. Some prefer the term "housemates" to "roommates" or "tenants." You may also hear the return of the word "boarders" to describe people who pay to live in a house. While this may conjure scenes from the Great Depression, it also conveys an economically sound concept of shar-ing a home. It creates a micro-community by providing private rooms for individuals.

Some people seek roommates for space they already have in their homes. Others are looking for people to buy into a home. A recent article[8] from CVT news in Canada talks about a woman, Janette Ledwith, who is doing just that. She is selling shares of her home, which ends up costing far less than if someone wanted to buy an en-tire home. "Some of the people who have come recall living in com-munity earlier in their life. For example at a university, where there are a number of people living together, and describing it as: 'it was the best time of my life when I had other people around,'[9] she says with a smile. "Here we are coming full circle." Janette is using a real estate agent to help her sell shares.

It appears that people have been doing this sort of thing under the radar for some time. The expression "where there's a will, there's a way" certainly applies. For example, we found an interesting story of a person in the Boston area who has been homesharing. She wrote about her experience in the Comment section in the New York Times in an article on cohousing.[10] The commenter said, "We have a tiny cohousing thing going on in our house. My housemate and I were friends from college and decided to split a two-family house. There's some additional legal complexity, but it's been great for 17 years now. We have one lawnmower too. And when I tell my story, I find out that other people have done some other creative living arrangements too, that are non-traditional. It's expensive to live here and it makes sense for some situations. There's more variety out there than people realize and it can work if done right. I wish there was a bit more acceptance of it in banking and law, though." When asked to specify her legal arrangements, she replied, "We have it set up as tenants-in-common, and drew up a legal document that gives each other the right to buy the other out first if that situation arose. We co-signed the mortgage and just split the annual deduction. There was only one time the IRS got confused on this but it was handled quickly. We have also agreed to let each other live out in the house without our heirs selling it as long as the other chooses to stay there. But we would like to put more legal protection around that in our wills and are trying to figure out how exactly that needs to be tidied up." This type of set-up could vary from state to state. But these ideas could be the launching pad that some need to get started on their own homesharing arrangements.

LOOKING BACK DARKLY...AND FORWARD!

Some of us may approach homesharing with trepidation. We may only have had experience with living under one roof with non-relatives when we were young adults or in college. Leslie remembers a time in her early 20's when she literally moved 4 times in a year because of crazy roommates and apartment issues. It was a good method of downsizing. However, it took a lot of energy that is plentiful when you are 23, but may not be in great supply if you are 74. You want your home situation to work out well. Theoretically, you know that if you are a renter and things don't work out, you can move. But that is something that you would like to avoid at this age and not do over and over again.

The good news is that as we grow older, we gain knowledge with experience. It may have been many decades since you have pondered what you want to look for and avoid in a roommate situation. We think it is helpful (and maybe a little amusing) to hear about what young, college-age roommates deal with as they navigate this for the first time. Perhaps this will remind you of what it was like when you were younger, and how much wiser you are as an adult. There are some valuable general pointers that are useful for a person of any age to consider as they look for a roommate.

Jennifer Birchim is a manager with the University of California Santa Barbara Community Housing Office. As with many campuses these days, in California and in other parts of the country, off-campus housing is incredibly crowded and understocked. Very few college students can afford to have just one roommate and are often living in small two bedroom apartments with five or more roommates. You can imagine how squabbles in these tight spaces with young people with little experience in conflict resolution can result in a huge mess. Jenn and her team deal with these issues with students every day. We asked her to tell us about it and offer some advice for older adults returning to the roommate life.

You deal with college roommates and their conflicts daily. What are some of the most common issues that you hear about?
The top roommate conflict issues are – overnight guests, food sharing, cleaning, and parking spaces. There are heavier conflicts associated with mental health and alcohol and drug use often when the roommates are concerned about one of their roommates. With these conflicts we utilize other campus departments like Student Mental Health, Distressed Students, CARE (Campus Advocacy, Resources & Education office), Alcohol and Drug program and CAPS (Counseling

& Psychological Services) to help with outreach to the student of concern.

What are the most resolvable issues for roommates?
Anything is resolvable as long as all of the parties are willing to come forward and have an open conversation about the issue. I often find that if everyone is willing to take responsibility for their part of a problem then they can willingly work through anything and come to a compromise. Most often the "issue" is usually not where the problem is stemming from – we call this the "who used my peanut butter" scenario – it blows up when you find someone used your peanut butter, but as we begin to talk about it, the issue is not with the peanut butter at all but with things that have piled up over time and it just exploded. Or we call it the garbage pile – and after a while it just smells so bad, you all can't take it anymore – and as we unlayer the garbage pile, we unearth a lot of unexpressed feelings about things that have been happening that no one has discussed.

What conflicts between roommates are simply not going to get better?
Again, any conflict is resolvable as long as all of the parties are willing to come forward and have an open honest conversation and both are willing to compromise. Often if one of the parties is not willing to budge, then there is not a conversation to be had because there is no willingness to move forward. In cases like this, then the other party has options to move out, find a replacement or find ways to deal with whatever issue is at hand – same with the other party who is unwilling to compromise.

Is it an advantage for roommates to know each other well before moving in together or can relative strangers make good roommates too?
I tell students that the person you party with is not often the best roommate. I think it is important to have honest conversations BEFORE you move in with potential roommates about things that mean the most to you whether that be cleaning, sleeping habits, overnight guests, lifestyle, etc. Often strangers who become roommates find great matches and live well together, but conversely, I have also seen matches that are terrible. There needs to be a willingness of both parties to bend one way or another in shared living situations and/or be open and honest

about what your expectations are. I think often people don't communicate about their communication style and that is where we see passive aggressive behavior or things are taken out of context. Be open about how you prefer to communicate – in person, phone, text, a note – and then you know and it is clear so that things are not taken out of context.

What do you recommend that potential roommates should learn about each other before committing to living together?
Schedules (night people, early morning people), overnight guests, parties, lifestyle questions (drug and alcohol use, pets, etc), cleaning (expectations), parking spaces and how that works, storage areas and how they are divided, utilities and how those are collected and charged.

What are the red flags of potentially bad roommates that students encounter? How do you advise them to steer clear of certain people?
I think everyone has their own best answers and I really try to tell people to trust their intuition. Often they go visit a place and then connect back with me. If they are hemming and hawing about certain things they saw that didn't feel right or sit right and then they start saying things like "well, I guess I can deal with that" or "I don't think that will bother me that much" or "maybe I can get used to that," I usually tell them those are red flags to me, that maybe they should keep looking. There are going to be priorities and things you aren't going to want to compromise that may go against your values or ethics and then there are things that are more negotiable – would be nice but not going to make or break (the situation). It is always a good time to tune in with yourself and check in with what things mean the most and what you are not willing to compromise. I think when people are stressed they make rash decisions. So I try to encourage people to really tune in and think about the choices they are making and not to rush into something that doesn't feel right.

Students connect online significantly more these days than any previous generation. Any tips for seniors who might be hesitant about finding roommates online?
I think the best advice is that if it is too good to be true it probably is. Proceed with caution, don't ever pay money before seeing a

place and always meet someone in person and do your research before agreeing to anything. Always get everything in writing, don't pay anything in cash and social media doesn't lie so if you can, check their online profiles to get a better sense of who they are. Don't rush into anything and be sure to do your research – if you don't have access to social media then find someone who can help you.

How do you think college-age students who are living on their own for the first time can inform baby boomers seeking new living arrangements?
Educate yourself about your rights and responsibilities both as a tenant and a landlord. Be sure to know what your non-negotiables are, what you are looking for, and also that your first choice might not be available. Think about what you are willing to compromise and what you are not. Utilize resources available to you and when you don't know then ask or find answers! READ YOUR LEASE and always know what you are signing. Go in with an open mind and heart and always trust your instincts.

I encourage students to ask for references even if you are the one who is renting the space. Talk to renters who have stayed there before and get an idea of how their stay was. If it is a sublease or something with a management company, I encourage renters to call the company and make sure that there haven't been any issues and that the rent is current. We had one instance with an international student who paid money to stay in a sublease. The second day he was there he got an eviction notice due to late rent by the previous tenants. It was so sad and we worked with the legal resource center to help him out and find him an alternative living situation.

I also know of many students who get stressed and then dive into a situation that might not be the best fit but out of stress they sign onto a lease and then are back in my office stressed about their living situation and wanting to get out of the lease. Then there are tenants who want something so specific and are having a really hard time finding something to fit their needs and that is when we work on re-evaluating what is the most important and non-negotiables and what they are willing to compromise on.

There are so many scenarios and I feel like I see a lot in our office but really it comes down to:

- educate yourself on the rights and responsibilities
- do your leg work
- do not make decisions under stress
- and really trust your instincts

HOMESHARING WITH A TWIST

Not everyone wants to move. If you have been "home proud" and kept up good home maintenance, you may not want to sell and hand over your creation to someone else. At the same time, you may need a little extra income or some added activity and purpose in your life.

Homesharing is when you find a housemate to either live in a room in your present home, or you move into a room in their house. This arrangement would involve a standard lease, usually for one year. If things work out, one would expect to renew the lease on a regular basis. This choice provides the opportunity for housemates to get to know each other, develop supportive relationships over time and reduce loneliness.

Perhaps you live in your own home and you have an extra furnished bedroom. The idea of committing to a roommate and locking into a lease for a year scares you. What if it doesn't work out? Twelve months is a long time to put up with a bad situation. You are curious and would love to give it a test run. What if you want a housemate for a shorter-term?

One solution is starting a short term stay rental in your home, such as with Airbnb and Vrbo. That can be great, especially if you enjoy meeting people from all over the world. With the short term stay, you will need to be on your toes managing guest reservations, keeping up with a possibly frequent guest turnover, cleaning, and upkeep. It requires some work to make your online offering desirable to potential guests. This can be a good fit for the right person.

MIMI'S STORY

When Mimi was in middle age, working and raising her two children with her husband, her vision of her old age was simple. "I thought that I would grow old alongside my husband. We loved each other and it would be a loss for either of us when the first one passed. We talked about how the other would survive and maybe even find another person." But, Mimi says that it didn't work out that way. Her children grew up and left the nest. Her marriage ended abruptly and badly. She was completely thrown off guard. In the months that followed, she was mourning the loss of her life relationship, she was in a job that didn't fit well and she needed to get out of town. So, she did. Mimi found good renters for her three bedroom home, bought an RV and hit the road. She traveled for 13 months across North America, exploring the US, Mexico and finally Canada. Everywhere that she went, she met wonderful people to talk with, fellow travelers and people in different locales and cultures. She was fascinated and enjoyed every minute.

On her return, she knew that she wanted to do something different. She was now 66 years old and did not feel compelled to return to full-time work. She saw her lovely three bedroom home with gorgeous mountain views in a new light. She had been living in a tiny RV quite comfortably for over a year. Coming home, her home felt enormous and empty. She missed meeting a variety of people and learning new things every day. As an experienced traveler, she understood that she had something special to offer others.

Mimi became an Airbnb host. She has two bedrooms that she offers and plenty of shared space, indoors and out for guests to enjoy. She asks every guest to put a pin on a world map in her hallway to note where they call home. She has now had over 200 guests in a year and a half. Her eyes light up talking about her guests and offering them her hospitality. "It feels good to me to help people and to get to know them." She has beautiful photos around her home of birds from near and far. Asked if there had been any problem guests, Mimi smiles diplomatically. "Let me put it this way. Out of over 200 guests, there have been only two that I would not welcome back. That's not so bad, is it?"

For Mimi, this venture has provided income and a sense of purpose.

HOST AN INTERNATIONAL STUDENT

Another alternative is to be a host to an international student in your home. These international students are typically young people of high school or college age. They are coming from other countries to the US to study for a semester or a school year or more. Most have studied some English and are glad for the opportunity to practice the language. In most cases, the host is paid to provide room and board. This includes a furnished room and meals. With older students, the host may provide food but not prepare meals. This is an excellent choice for those who are intrigued by people of other cultures and want to introduce a young person to ours.

Here is an interview with Beth, age 58, who is married with one college-aged son still living at home. She has been hosting international students in her home for about 20 years and plans to continue when she retires. She lives in a five bedroom house and currently has two long term international college students living in the home.

What do you most enjoy about doing this?
We all enjoy the interaction. Also having guests helps us appreciate our home and area with fresh eyes, to use the house and enjoy sights and activities to the fullest.

What are some of the problems or challenges that you have experienced hosting college exchange students in your home?
I could write a book. (I am! lol) Seriously there are always problems living with people even those you know and love, much less strangers coming from another culture. But as with an international marriage, those differences are not a surprise, so we can anticipate them. I do often get irritated, but I feel I have become a pro at problem-solving. One example: I tend to get frustrated when I feel ignored when people don't follow the rules and systems I have in place to make group living work. So I have color-coded messages and instructions that I leave around. White labels (I usually use electrical tape) are for welcome messages, offers, and friendly communication. Yellow is for instructions, cautions, and requests. I also do a lot of texting with photographs about scheduling, food, etc., and impress upon them the importance of letting me know if they understand.

How do you see incorporating hosting college students in your retirement? Will you do things differently?

The way that we host has transitioned with each phase of our family life. (We started) first with au pairs when our kids were small, then kids their age in high school, now back to college students. I am currently working toward more independent guests. The pressure to provide food was no longer worth the compensation difference for meals included, so for current guests the condition was access to staple foods and 2-4 shared dinner invites per week, but no guaranteed meals. The challenge here has been that they are Japanese guys like my husband, and he tends to feel sorry for them if I don't feed them regularly. My solution for this was to let them know what I'd be cooking in advance at least three times a week, so if they want to plan their week around that they can. They don't cook much for themselves, even though my son often does and he is a role model for them in other ways. It happens that these two guys come from plenty of money and their parents appreciate us as hosts, so I don't feel as responsible as I might for students with fewer resources.

Is it costly? Are you reimbursed or do the students pay rent? In other words, would a senior hosting a student expect to make any income doing this or would they do it for the other benefits (decrease social isolation, learn about other cultures, etc)?
We are in an area that attracts a lot of international students, and where one-bedroom apartments start at $1500/month, so we are definitely reimbursed. The current rate is $900/mo, with all utilities, furnished rooms, toiletries, etc. Seniors could get fair compensation in most areas that attract students.

What would your advice be for seniors considering this option?
Starting out it is best to go through an agency or a reputation-based homesharing app. I use some apps and websites such as homestay-finder.com and homestayweb.com. You can also contact local language schools or (colleges or universities) with international programs and ask which agencies they deal with.

Are there characteristics of people who make good hosts to exchange students? Are there people, in your view, who would not do well with this?
The easiest answer is not people who are doing it only for the money.

It never works out. Open-minded, flexible, friendly people will enjoy the experience and be better hosts for guests who are facing the challenges of living in a new country. Most want a chance to practice English, so they will appreciate hosts who are available to interact, even if the arrangement doesn't include meals.

BECOME A HOMESTAY HOST

According to Homestay.com[11], a homestay is "staying in a spare room of a real home while the homeowner is there. All around the world, from cities to off the beaten path destinations, homestays are a type of accommodation that defines the phrase a 'home from home'. In a homestay, you book to stay with a local in their home. They are your 'host' during your stay." In contrast with a short term rental, such as Airbnb, a homestay can be a few days or a couple of months. They attract international students, world travelers, people who are moving from one country to another.

LIKE TINDER FOR HOMESHARERS? ONLINE SERVICES HELP FIND THE PERFECT MATCH

Let's say you are ready to take the plunge. Now what? The idea of putting yourself out there as a roommate may be intimidating. When Amanda was younger she did not follow Jennifer's advice above. Her attitude was: "throw caution to the wind!" As we get older, that philosophy doesn't work any longer. This is where homeshare services can be invaluable. The National Shared Housing Resource Center has homesharing listed by state but there are currently only 16 states listed.

One example is **Senior Homeshares**. This is a description of how they match homeowners with other seniors looking for affordable housing: "Senior Homeshares is, at its core, a matching service. Homeowners and home-seekers each fill out a personal profile, which includes much the same information that any roommate would want to know. It also adds some questions that are unique to older users. We also encourage users to add introductory text of their own, to share hobbies, special considerations, etc." Senior Homeshares also provides links to sample homeshare agreements. There is no cost to use their service.

Silvernest is another homesharing service. The homeowner pays a monthly fee and the potential renter pays nothing unless they would like to enhance their appeal with pre-screening and a background check for $29.99. To give an idea of availability, a search in the San Francisco bay area yielded about 56 potential sharing opportunities. By comparison, Minneapolis, Minnesota has about 16 and Salt Lake City has two. Availability varies greatly, but if the projected growth trend continues, additional homes should be added.

INTO THE WEEDS OF LEGAL AGREEMENTS

We are not attorneys or landlords and so can't give legal advice! However, we strongly recommend getting legal advice on the different types of living arrangements. Get legal documents to protect yourself whether you are home buy sharing, renting to others or renting from someone else. Here are a few things to consider:

IF YOU ARE RENTING FROM SOMEONE ELSE

- Is your agreement month to month or for a defined period of time? (For example six months or a year). This can be very important if you have to leave the residence due to illness, rehab or even if you don't like it anymore! With a long term lease agreement, you may be responsible financially for the duration of the lease if you leave early.
- Is there a security deposit and is it refundable? Can you sublease if you need to make a permanent or temporary move?
- What is the expected increase in rent? Is this spelled out in the rental agreement or is a rate increase up to the landlady or landlord?
- What are the rules of the household? Everything from pets, smoking, noise and overnight guests.

IF YOU ARE RENTING TO OTHERS

- Determine the kind of rental agreement you want. Spell out all rules, deposits, utilities, and maintenance.

- Be aware of federal and state laws regarding discrimination based on skin color, religion, disability, sexual orientation.
- How do you evict someone if you need to?
- What about damage incurred to your property by a tenant. How do you handle that?
- Are you covered by your home insurance if you have a tenant? Insist that your tenant have their own renter's insurance.
- How will you handle roommate disputes?

CO-OWNING A HOME

We found some sound advice that we share below from the legal advice website, Nolo.com. Their mission is to help consumers and small businesses find answers to their everyday legal and business questions. Keep in mind that legal housing arrangements vary from state to state. It is imperative that you consult a real estate attorney in your state to make sure your bases are covered.

"Co-owning a home can be a great idea. But again, consult a realtor or real estate attorney to make sure that everyone is legally covered. When you buy a home with others, you are entering into a living arrangement and a legal relationship as well. How you own a home together determines how you can get financing, and what your rights and responsibilities are. Things to consider are to whom you can each sell or leave your share of the property, and more. Homeownership is governed by local and state laws so any advice we give is generic. Some local municipalities have strict laws governing the number of unrelated people that can live in the same house."

Here are some of the possible legal arrangements for co-ownership of a home as described on the Nolo.com[12] website. Take legal precautions by consulting a real estate attorney in your area.

TENANCY IN COMMON (TIC)

"When you own property as tenants in common (TIC), you each own an undivided share. For example, if you own a duplex with another person as tenants in common, you each own a portion of the *whole* building. Even though each of you may live in and maintain one of the units. TICs are customarily used when two or more unrelated people own a home together and are also frequently used in multi-unit residential buildings, such as a duplex or triplex."

JOINT TENANCY

"Joint tenancy is a form of ownership that includes a right of survivorship. When one owner dies, that person's share of the property passes automatically to the other owner(s). In contrast, a TIC share goes to the owner's heirs at death. Joint tenancy is most often used by couples and families. But, it could also work well for unrelated owners in a small shared housing arrangements who want the security of knowing that their interests in the property will be protected if another owner dies.

Forming a joint tenancy usually requires that all owners have equal interests in the property and that they acquired title at the same time, on the same title document. Most joint tenancies are financed with a single shared mortgage."

LIMITED LIABILITY COMPANY (LLC)

"In the process of developing shared housing, such as cohousing, many groups form a limited liability company (LLC) that holds title to the property. By forming an LLC, the group becomes a legal entity and can enter into contracts. This allows it to purchase land and partner with developers and contractors. The LLC form of ownership also provides liability protection to individual group members, should anything go wrong during the development process."

The same details and issues that govern rental properties also apply to homeownership.

- What are the rules of the household?
- How are utilities split among homeowners?
- What if someone needs to leave temporarily due to illness, rehab, a family crisis or other problem? Can they sublet their room?
- How are group decisions made? For example, what if there

is conflict or strong disagreement among owners? Is there a process for handling these potential problems?

WHAT'S IT REALLY LIKE: OPENING YOUR HOME TO HOUSEMATES

We interviewed Stephanie, a divorced woman in her 70's. After surviving a difficult divorce in her late 40's, Stephanie hadn't really given thought to what it would be like to become an empty nester. Then, after her children had grown and flown the coop, she was left with a three bedroom house...all alone. One of her bedrooms is on the basement level with its own bath and entrance. It became clear that she could benefit financially from renting that out and still have a lot of privacy. She relied mostly on word of mouth with friends and soon she found a renter. Over time, she realized that she enjoyed having some company around and thought she would take the risk to expand her household.

She decided to rent out the second bedroom. Because there are two additional bathrooms, one on the main floor and one upstairs, she lets the housemate have the main floor bathroom and the upstairs bathroom is reserved for herself. "The kitchen is small, so cooking can be an issue, but so far, it has always worked out. My housemates don't seem to cook as much as I do."

Stephanie has been sharing her house with housemates for over ten years now. She has found them by asking friends if they know anyone looking for a house to share and it has been a good method. She found out about one person who was relocating to her part of the country. They met by Skype and worked out the details. She has had people that are close to her age and that has been fine.

Currently, she has a 28-year-old female housemate. Stephanie admits that having that younger energy around is fun. She has never had a male housemate except in the separate basement section of the house. When asked if there has ever been a problem with a housemate, Stephanie related this story. "I did have a male housemate once that didn't work out. Some neighbors invited us over shortly after he moved in. While we were there, I realized, and my friends realized, that there were just certain things about this fellow's need to control the conversation that made us uncomfortable. Shortly after that evening, I called my housemate at his work and told him that I didn't think it was a good fit. He agreed to move out." For Stephanie, experience has shown her that this is a practical way for her to be with others and save money. Ultimately, she is a realist. She is in good health now and hopes to continue. If, however, she finds herself not able to manage the house, she will move. In the meantime, she will continue to enjoy the company of her housemates.

WHAT HAPPENED TO STEPHANIE WHEN COVID HIT?

We checked back with Stephanie in June 2020 to find out what the impact of COVID has been on her homesharing situation. "It's been complicated." She describes how things have evolved with each of her housemates. Her 28 year old roommate, Pamela, had to deal with sheltering in place and working remotely. "Pamela has a boyfriend who has been here a lot. She has been off work, and working from home; for the last month she's been on un-employment, so has been around. The boyfriend works in Sports Medicine, so, though they sort of shut down for a month or two, he has had some exposure. He has been pretty good about wear-ing masks, etc. And she has been careful with handwashing, etc. We sanitize the doorknob daily, and so on. But, I'd say we've been lucky! It has felt a bit awkward, at times, especially to have the boyfriend around. But I've been somewhat relaxed about it myself. (I'm not really responsible for anyone else, so that allows me to have a slightly fatalistic attitude. I just worry about being a vector for others). Since our county has definitely flattened the curve, and is slowly opening up, I think we just have to be very attentive to exposure now."

Stephanie goes on to describe a very different situation with her other housemate, Lauren, who lives downstairs. "She went to Spain for 6 months in December, and a friend sublet. Cassie, the friend, works as a hospital chaplain, so she is subject to exposure. She also has been cohabiting often with her boyfriend who lives in town. So,

Cassie was not around a lot, and when she was here, she was extremely careful. She has not come down with COVID."

"Lauren returned from Spain last week. In Spain, she had been isolated in her apartment for the last several months. Then, she was quite sick for a couple of weeks in March, and eventually had tested positive for COVID. She has kept distance from us, although we see each other and have conversations. Her main concern is that she was on a very crowded flight on return to the US. She worries about what she may transmit from that. Of course, we don't know if, or how long, one has COVID immunity."

PROS AND CONS OF HOMESHARING

PROS:

1. Financial flexibility. Women, in particular, may have lower incomes as they get older. If they have not been in the workforce or have had to take significant time off, their retirement income may be limited. Sharing living space can have significant savings advantages. Whether you are sharing the costs of owning or renting, it will be less expensive than having your own place.
2. Community/Socialization. Loneliness is a growing problem among older adults. Banding together in a common living space can provide companionship and camaraderie as well as emotional support. Emotional connection can be enhanced with something as simple as someone acknowledging you and saying good morning.
3. Sharing a home may have the additional benefit of allowing you to live in a space that is much nicer than you could have afforded on your own. You may be able to live in a house instead of an apartment.
4. Increased Opportunities and Shaking up the Routine: When you spend more time with others, you may find yourself doing things that are new to you. For example, you may be in the habit of doing your grocery shopping at the same store

every week. A housemate might invite you to join her at a weekly farmer's market that you have never been to. She says she gets the best tomatoes there. You may have always thought it was too much bother to add another errand, but find that you enjoy the open air and community atmosphere.

5. Brain Stimulation. There is nothing more boring and mind-numbing than sitting alone staring at the same four walls, or worse, a TV blaring all day. Having a real live person walk through and engage in conversation exercises a different part of your brain.

6. Sharing skills and abilities. Some homesharers trade with each other. One of you may have a car and still drives. That person drives the other to the store. The other person makes a superb lasagna and creates a Sunday dinner for both to share.

7. Security. It's nice to know that you could leave for a weekend to visit your best friend from high school. Your housemate will be at your home holding down the fort. If you lock yourself out of the house and can't find your keys, you have another person to call who can let you in.

CONS:

1. A roommate situation can be too much togetherness for some people. Unlike most cohousing, where most people own their own space (with private kitchen, bathroom, etc.) sharing a house means you will have your own room. Yet you will share in the other amenities. Privacy may be an issue for some in this situation.

2. Some do not care for rules and regulations at home. Homesharing works best if rules and agreements are spelled out in advance. These include the financial details, household responsibilities, legal arrangement, smoking, and overnight guest policy.

3. Health problems. What happens if someone needs more physical or mental assistance than what can be provided? How are decisions made? Stairs may not be a problem when you move in, but changing health status could impact that.

4. What if people don't get along? You can't always know, even by an initial meeting, if there will be compatibility. How will this be handled? Possible areas of conflict are pets, cleanliness, temperature, noise, and assigned chores.

5. Not all houses are created equal: A ranch house may more likely be on one level making mobility accessible. That could work for a group living situation. But, other features of a house could be more challenging. A house in certain suburban neighborhoods may not be close enough to bus lines or medical clinics for an older adult to easily get to where they need to go. Or, you simply may not like the cramped, small child's bedroom converted to a rental.

IS GOLDEN GIRLS (OR BOYS!) RIGHT FOR YOU?

THIS IS FOR YOU IF:

- You enjoy the company of strangers and all that comes with it. That includes a comfort level with people not of your own choosing or even the same values.
- You are comfortable living with people in close quarters and don't mind sharing common space like a single kitchen.
- Rules are not a concern for you. The more clearly rules are spelled out the better!
- Legal transactions don't scare you. Rental or home buying agreements are familiar to you.

STAY CLEAR IF:

- Living in close quarters gives you the jitters! You don't like to share your space and privacy is very important to you.
- You don't like to be told what and what not to do.
- Signing lease agreements or home buying documents makes you feel trapped. If things don't work out, you want a quick exit without any legal consequences.
- Rules? Those are for children. Adults can work these things out amongst themselves, right?

4

THE FAMILY TRADITION-
MOVING IN WITH THE KIDS

Moving in with the kids used to be a time honored tradition. Now, with people living longer and the cost of assisted living and nursing care skyrocketing, more families are considering this option. When Amanda was growing up, her grandfather died when she was about ten years old. Her grandmother moved in so the family could take care of her. She didn't own a home and only had social security to live on. In the 1960's women of that age (she was in her 70's) were much less likely to be self-sufficient, or have their own income. Perhaps they only worked a few years and had very little social security since they raised families. Plus there were no "retirement" communities. The decision was a necessity.

It would seem that this necessity is coming full circle. As fewer people are able to afford assisted living or private care in the home, families are banding together to help one another. They are doing so for a variety of reasons. Sometimes circumstances create the perfect environment in which to make a decision that benefits everyone. Barbara's story is a perfect example of that.

BARBARA'S STORY

Barbara is in her 70's and her husband became ill and was too much for her to handle. At the same time, her daughter was going through a divorce and they all decided together that her daughter and her daughter's sons would move in to help Barbara take care of her husband. Barbara's husband died 4 years ago.

How did you and your daughter decide to move in together?
I was retired when Bill (became) ill. The deciding factor in this decision was that my husband was ill with multiple health problems including COPD and lung issues, and as my daughter Lorraine was recently divorced with two sons it was the perfect solution for her to move in. The decision came easily to us and it also made my husband very happy. I needed the help and she was willing to help.

How did you and your daughter decide on caregiving tasks between you?
In terms of caregiving duties, we didn't really discuss the details, it just seemed to happen naturally and we both did our part. Lorraine worked so she took over when she got home.

What about other contributions such as rent, utilities and household tasks?
Lorraine contributes financially and she likes doing housework so that was a bonus! I helped take care of the boys by taking them to and from school. Lorraine supported me when my husband would get irritated. I was close to my husband and as the primary caregiver he sometimes took out his frustrations on me. My daughter was the buffer between us. That helped a lot.

Did you and your daughter ever consider hiring outside help?
My husband was getting to the point where we would have needed help. At the end he was on oxygen. I was so grateful to Lorraine and my other two children for being there for me. Between us all, there was always someone with him in the hospital during those times that he had to go.

Were there ever humorous moments?
There were numerous moments because as a family we laugh a lot and try to look on the bright side by the grace of God. My two daughters and myself are very spiritual and feel a closeness to God. That has sustained us through this process.

A friend of mine is caring for her Mother who is in her 90's, she has home care too so gets a couple of hours off during the week. I was blessed with a closeness to my children who are always willing to help me whereas my friend is doing this on her own.

Your husband died four years ago. Your family has been through so much, but it sounds like the situation of all of you living together worked really well. Reflecting back, what do you think helped?
I feel because my personality is laid back and I go with the flow plus a very strong spiritual nature, it really helped me. Also my husband was very close to the younger of my daughter's sons and that helped him immensely. Also neither of my grandsons were unruly or mouthy but very respectful and are very nice to be around.

My daughter and the boys are still with me. I am 72 and retired. I'm pretty healthy and try to stay active. My oldest grandson attends university not far from here and the younger one attends a private school close by. They are amazing boys and my daughter is awesome. I also had another grandson living with me for a couple of years as I'm closer to his university, he is living in residence now and graduates in 2020, where does the time go! I have been blessed with an awesome family who for the most part all get along. There would be something amiss if we were so perfect we never had differences from time to time. I am so grateful to God for them and all my children and grandchildren.

THE MULTIGENERATIONAL ADVANTAGE

It is not unusual to see multigenerational families living together. Parents live with their kids and their own parents all together. In some cases grandkids live with grandparents as well. "A Pew Research Center survey[13] finds that nearly 79 million adults in the United States, or 31.9 percent of the adult population, live in a "shared household," meaning a home in which two or more adults not intimately attached live in the same home." AARP found that the share of multigenerational households (defined as including two or more adult generations, or grandparents and grandchildren younger than 25) rose from a low of 12% in 1980 to 20% in 2016.[14]

And then you have adult kids moving back in with their parents as well! According to the Pew Research Center: "In recent years, young adults have been the age group most likely to live in multigenerational households (previously, it had been adults ages 85 and older). Among 25- to 29-year-olds in 2016, 33% were residents of such households. Among a broader group of young adults, those ages 18 to 34, living with parents surpassed other living arrangements in 2014 for the first time in more than 130 years."[15]

The AARP policy institute found that half of caregivers report that their care recipient lives in the recipient's own home. More than one in three say their recipient lives in the caregiver's household (35%). Higher-hour caregivers are predominantly living with their care recipient (62%), while lower-hour caregivers are more likely to report their care recipient lives in his or her own home (57%), or in a facility or community with varying degrees of care support (14 percent in nursing or long-term care, assisted living, or independent living or retirement community)."[16]

There are cultural determinants on whether caregivers are likely to live with their relatives. In the same AARP report 43% of Hispanic caregivers and 45% of Asian Americans report cohabitation as compared with 34% white and 28% African American.

INTERVIEW WITH MARY

Mary is 78-year-old living in a mid-sized city in the west. She embodies the reverse trend in caregiving. She is taking care of her adult daughter who is disabled. Here is her story:

How did you end up in senior housing?
I left a rural area to move to the city. Aging in place in a rural community became harder and harder. If I had more family support I could see staying there. Taking care of a 100 year old home and the land became too much.

I thought, if I don't move now, when am I going to do it? I found subsidized housing in the city which allowed me the freedom not to think about maintenance and yard care. So I moved in. The rent was raised recently. I have a 2 bedroom with views which is $1000 a month. I would not be able to find anything in the city more reasonable than that.

I have no responsibilities. I don't worry about maintenance, parking, or pay for utilities. I have cheap covered parking for $15 a month.

Pets are allowed so I have a little dog. There are two social workers on site that help people connect with resources. There are no organized activities, but there is transportation once a week for shopping. Any activities are organized by the residents.

How did you end up taking care of your daughter?
My daughter got sick and I had to move her in with me. She has myopathy, necrotic myatosis and mental health problems. For a while she couldn't walk at all. She was in a nursing home. I eventually moved her in with me so I could take care of her. She was treated with anti-cancer chemo medications that ruined her esophagus. Her digestive system is messed up. She now has to use a walker and is on several medications. Fortunately, she is on Medicaid and Medicare. If she had to go to a nursing home, Medicaid would pay for that. Her only income is disability – $900 a month. She can contribute a little to our household expenses.

How do you feel about your daughter living with you?
I didn't want to do it but I wouldn't have it any other way. I had no choice. I would prefer to live alone. The social aspect of senior living isn't as important to me. I don't need the social aspect that senior living offers. But the ease of living there allows me to take care of my daughter.

What would you do if you needed more care?
I am worried about it, but only as it affects my daughter. Who will take care of her when I am gone? I haven't thought about what would happen if I become disabled. I have only been worried about my daughter. I am looking at ways she can be cared for after I am gone.

I do have good insurance. I have Medicare with a secondary that pays for everything and I feel secure in what that offers me.

I worry and I want to make sure things are secure for her. Living with my daughter is complicated because I was a bad mom. I was an alcoholic. Emotionally I was not a good mom. I took care of my granddaughter who was into drugs. My alcoholism affected my daughter. My daughter is grateful because she always thought she would take care of me. She gets tired but she does what she can for me. She cleans house and keeps to herself. I am in charge and she knows that and respects that. She stays at home and doesn't socialize.

We have separate bedrooms. I don't feel like I owe her anything. I just feel like this is my responsibility to her. She stays out of my way. I do what I want and she acquiesces to me.

It's not a bother for me and I am glad I could do it for her. She is very mindful of my space. She isn't entitled and she is grateful. The alternative is not good for her. We try to be honest with each other. We had a lot of work to do with one another due to her childhood and my bad parenting. I had to work to get her into senior housing with me since she is 52 which is younger than the required age. But I fought for her.

I feel fortunate. This is not how I imagined my old age, but this is the way it is. I plan on staying where I am because my daughter feels secure. I never really thought about me.

A LESSON LEARNED FROM HER PARENTS: CREATING A MASTER PLAN

When Maureen and her husband first moved to the Rocky Mountains, they were enthralled by the beauty of nature and the wonderful outdoor activities. Soon they were enjoying skiing, biking, windsurfing and the magnificent rugged scenery.

However, as many locals learn, there are some hidden risks for certain individuals to living in this high-altitude naturescape. Salt Lake City, in particular, has an unfortunate air pollution problem. The combination of increasing car emissions with industry pollution, produces high particulate matter in the air as well as high ozone levels. For some people, living in this high-altitude environment with excessive pollution levels can cause or worsen serious health problems.

Maureen had never been a smoker. She had always been involved in high fitness and athletic activities throughout her life before and after moving to Utah. But after decades of living in this state, Maureen developed troubling respiratory problems. It began with asthma which then developed into emphysema. When she is up in the mountains enjoying her favorite activity, skiing, the air is relatively clear and she is okay. But down in the city, the pollutants gather. Maureen has a medical HEPA filter system in her home. She has adapted her schedule to be out and about earlier in the day when pollution levels are lower. She has an entire wardrobe of air filtration masks for the high level days. But she still suffers greatly.

Maureen grew up on the east coast in a large, loving family. Her parents, ahead of their time and their thinking, always had what they referred to as their "Master Plan." They decided early in their retirement to downsize. They gathered their adult children, told them to take furniture, artwork, and any other household goods that they wanted to have from the big family home where they had grown up. The rest they donated to the Catholic Church. The parents then moved to a much smaller home. And, some years later, they did it again. As their health declined, they chose a single floor condominium that would better meet their needs as they aged. They freely discussed with their children their spirituality and religious beliefs, and their thoughts about their own healthcare and death and dying. "We talked about everything in our family." Everyone was more or less on the same page. Her parents lived to a good old age, though they did suffer with chronic illness. But Maureen is certain that they lived it with their choices intact.

After going through a difficult divorce and in her 40's, Maureen decided that it was time to downsize. She sold her single family home and moved with her 12 year old daughter to a smaller square footage townhouse. She continued working, and retired at 65. By then her respiratory illnesses had emerged.

Meanwhile, her daughter, Evelyn, had completed graduate school and married. She and her husband had moved to a charming town in New England. Maureen went to visit and fell in love with the town. There were flat biking trails everywhere. There was beautiful scenery without the high altitude. And she was close enough to her east coast hometown to go visit her siblings and do sightseeing in Boston and New York City.

Maureen and her daughter began to talk about the future. Evelyn and her husband invited Maureen to come live with them. But, Maureen wanted to make sure to respect their space. "I've never wanted to be a burden to my family." Their rental home at the time only had one bathroom. Maureen said "they thought it was fine, but I knew better. That was just too close for comfort."

But the talks continued. After Maureen had returned to Salt Lake City, her daughter and son-in-law announced that they had found a house to purchase that had a mother-in-law apartment. The following summer when the ozone levels were uncomfortably high, Maureen went to stay with them for a month. "Even though I told them that I didn't want them to buy a house with me in mind, that I could just find a temporary place to rent nearby, I really had to admit that I loved the space that they had found." The mother-in-law apartment has terrific windows and enough space for a bedroom, bathroom and kitchenette. A bonus is that it is all on one floor with outdoor access, universally designed door openings and an accessible shower. Maureen and her daughter are enjoying designing the interior together. She has gifted some money to them toward the house payment. Maureen has insisted on paying a monthly rent when she is there. She has her mail forwarded from her permanent address in Utah to her New England address during the time that she is there.

Moving to New England permanently however, is not Maureen's choice at this time. She has a long-term relationship in Utah, a person who is the love of her life. They enjoy skiing, travel and other adventures together. Though he is active physically, he also has some serious medical issues to contend with. He has children and grandchildren from a previous marriage all close by. He has enjoyed staying with Maureen in New England, but will not be moving there. She has her townhouse which is comfortably set up for her medical needs at this point. But she looks forward to her time at lower altitude and with her daughter and son-in-law.

"I'm not ready to move there permanently. Maybe never. But it's wonderful that I can go there each summer and be with my family and feel at home. I'm so grateful that I had my parents as an example. They had their master plan, and I have mine."

EMBRACING CHANGE

"My life has been full of changes and that has made me a more resilient person."

Cindy lived in Mexico for 30 years with her husband. They were quasi-retired. When Cindy's husband died, her daughter who lives in North Carolina asked Cindy to move to North Carolina to be closer. At about the same time, her son moved from Thailand to North Carolina with his family. Her life has taken a pretty dramatic turn, but then again, Cindy's history if full of changes and adventures!

Cindy and her husband initially moved to Mexico for the tax benefit and although they loved many parts of the world, Mexico seemed like a good fit. It was close enough to their kids and friends and it was also affordable. The culture, ocean, art and cuisine were appealing. "We realized we were never going to return to ordinary life again."

When Cindy's husband died and her daughter invited her to live in North Carolina, Cindy decided to take yet another adventure. "I am living in sort of a family commune. The idea of living in a southern state didn't initially appeal to me. I thought it was pretty but wasn't sure I could live there." Cindy lives in a cottage where her daughter lives one street over. Cindy lives just a few steps from the "big house" on the same piece of property where her son and daughter in law and their kids live. The close proximity has not been a problem so far.

The conventional way most people would view this situation is that Cindy's family is there to provide her help and support. But, Cindy has found that she is needed in unexpected ways as well. "They do a lot to help me but I am helping them a lot. Since they don't have driver's licenses yet I am the one that helps my 16 year old grandson with driver's ed. We didn't anticipate how challenging life would be for my son and his family to move here. He doesn't have work history in the states. I have to be the designated supervisory driver for my grandson since the requirement is to have had a US driver's license for 3 years, which my son does not have. I also pick up my grandchildren from school. We are learning together."

As far as Cindy finding other opportunities to keep busy, she has approached this in the same way as everything else in her life. With purpose, intent and follow through. "My daughter told me to go find a MeetUp Group and "find some friends!" I had never heard of that, but did look at several groups and was so fortunate to find a group called "Coastal Women Over 50 Looking for Friends and Fun." Honestly, it was months before I thought about how much over 50 I was and how brave I was to put myself into this younger group! They are a very diverse and interesting group of women, with more social offerings than I want every week! Out of this group I am growing more personal friendships with a couple of women, which is nice."

When asked about the possibility of needing more help for herself in the future this is what Cindy has to say: "I had a group of friends who planned to live together, and take care of each other, but then one got Alzheimer's, another one's son died, and another's health started to decline and suddenly the idea completely fell apart."

"I think people have this idea that friends will take care of us, and it won't necessarily happen. I guess the same could be said of family too. My daughter told me when I moved to North Carolina people aren't going to come knocking on your door to make friends. So, you better figure it out. And that is what I have done."

"I go to an occasional lecture at the University, am teaching a cooking class every six weeks at a very nice cooking school in town and I have LOTS of company!!! LOTS!"

"I am also taking a group of women to Southeast Asia, again, in August and that will not only be fun, but keeps me very busy in the planning details in advance. I have a very full and rich life."

FAMILY COMES IN ALL SHAPES AND SIZES

Over the years, we have seen many combinations of people in a family home. We live in the age of blended families. Many people seeking to reduce isolation and costs become creative. For example:

- We knew one older divorced woman who had been married several times in her lifetime. After some health concerns, she decided to move in with her daughter and her family in another state. So did her first husband, the father of her daughter. It had been many years since their marriage. In fact, it had been decades since they had even seen each other. She had an upstairs bedroom in her daughter's house. He had the basement bedroom and bathroom. They got along fine.
- One fellow in his 70's had been heart-broken when his wife of many years up and left him for another man. She and her

"soulmate" moved across the country. He attempted to find another partner with poor results. He still lived in the large family home that he had shared with his ex-wife. Friends and family were concerned with him staying there, moping around and thinking about the past. He was still close to his ex-wife's brother and his wife. When his ex-in laws had some financial difficulties, he invited them to move into the big house with him. They were younger and were able to help him with the household chores and yard work. He enjoyed their company and felt less lonely.

ONE FAMILY, THREE GENERATIONS AND A BICOASTAL SOLUTION

Our favorite satellite radio host and dynamic speaker, Sandra Beck is a delight to talk with and to listen to. She has multiple audiences and shows, including Military Moms, DynamicWomen and Motherhood. Her message throughout is empowerment, delivered with empathy, creativity and a large dose of humor.

She is also an expert of living with a family of three generations. But, as with most things about Sandra's life, she does it with her own signature style.

After her mother passed away, she and her siblings pitched in to help their widowed dad. He wasn't doing well living alone in upstate New York. Sandra was recently divorced and raising her two young sons in California. She asked her dad if he would join her family and help her. At the time, he could drive and take the kids to school, babysit after school while she was working and he could hold down the fort when she left town for business. Her dad liked the idea, but was reluctant because he knew he would miss his friends and community.

Sandra's brother, who lives in dad's town, also had space available in his home for his father. Together they came up with a solution. Her dad would live with Sandra and the grandsons during the school year and spend the summers in his hometown living with his son. This way, he could stay connected with his friends, family and history in New York. And, at the same time, he had a unique opportunity to become a vital part of his daughter and grandchildren's lives across the country in California.

Sandra's dad has been doing this bicoastal, "living with the kids times two" arrangement for over 10 years now. Over that time, his health and abilities have changed. Now, his grandsons are teens and they help look after their granddad. Sandra is clear that the current arrangement may not last forever. But, for years now, the benefits have been many for all the members of the family in both states.

If this idea of sharing a loved elder between two households appeals to you, you may wonder about the logistics. How do you make it work without causing more stress? What if you are the senior? You may be concerned about how your needs will be met. When talking to Sandra, her love and respect for her father that is shared by her siblings and her children comes through loud and clear. That is vital to making this unique arrangement work. However, this plan would be a disaster if the older person involved were being treated like a hot potato, or only desired for the financial boost the social security check might add to an adult child's household.

Again, family communication and planning are key. Clear goals and expectations help. Sandra's dad and her family were willing to be flexible and try something different. Nothing is written in stone, but everyone has been open to make it work. Here, Sandra shares her tips for travel, the transition and keeping the senior member of the family happy and healthy:

1. **The Transition between Houses** – Pack the transition carry on/travel bag with their favorites as well as necessities so when they arrive they can immediately relax upon arrival. In my dad's rolling bag that goes on the plane with him, we include his medicine for five days, his fav socks and slippers, his fav PJs, sweatshirt, and robe. We ship/airline checked baggage things he wants at the next house that could get lost and/or replaced like his Matlock DVDs.

2. **What's My Dad's Normal**-We email ahead detailed instructions for care for my dad including favorite meals including the recipe, daily exercise, fav snacks, fav tv programs, what to watch out for (hiding chocolate in his room-sneaking soda-he is diabetic and how to spot when his blood sugar is too

high). What his normal sleep pattern is (it changes over time so you don't worry he's dead if he naps twice or three times a day or sleeps past 7 AM). Basically flag the next household as to what is his normal – left hip hurts, can't hear, won't wear mask or hearing aids. You fight the battles you can win.

3. **Dad's Routine** – Keep him on the same schedule as much as possible – that's huge...he gets calls from my uncle Gary at 1pm, my other brother at 4pm, my aunt at noon, sister at 10:30... and breakfast at 6:30/ his lunch is at 11:30/ his dinner at 4:30... popcorn and water after 7 or an apple – Those time stamps and those calls are vital to his mental health – so plan around them or accommodate them. Too much change or unfamiliar is scary. And for heaven's sake – don't buy anything other than HeadNShoulders and Dove soap or the world will end.

4. **Familiarity at Both Houses** – Keep both his rooms somewhat familiar – we have photos of the family, of my mom, a few navy things from his original home, blue his fav color, and a lazy boy in the room here in California and the room in NY and his own TV.

Sandra adds: "I find eldercare needs to be simple. Pay attention and talk to your senior. But when you blow a simple need, you are in for one ornery senior and he won't want to stay with you (so my other sisters and brothers found out when they want to do things their way hahahaha). Happy Senior, Happy Home."

PROS AND CONS OF MOVING IN WITH THE KIDS

PROS

- The most obvious advantage of living with children or grandchildren is the cost savings. Assisted living and independent living (depending on where you live) can be very expensive. According to Genworth, the median cost for assisted living across the country is $3,700 per month.[17] And that doesn't even take into account the added costs of care in assisted living. Sharing space reduces living expenses like rent and utilities which can be shared. If someone has personal care needs like help with dressing or bathing that can be provided by family, this too can be a big cost savings.

- Multi generations living together can help to combat ageism by familiarizing younger people with older relatives. There are opportunities for mentoring and learning across generations.
- The potential for reciprocal care. An older person helping to take care of younger generations provides a sense of purpose.
- Living together helps to combat loneliness, a significant problem as people age.

CONS

- Families often underestimate the time and effort it takes to care for an older adult. If an older family member already has chronic medical problems, these problems will likely worsen over time.
- What about home modifications? Moving someone in without adding safety features can cause more problems than you were hoping to solve in the first place! Consider stairs, lighting, grab bars, fall risk assessment, and doorway and hallway width in case a wheelchair is needed later.
- Togetherness is a good thing. Right? Well, yes. But all that togetherness may get on people's nerves. There are space and privacy concerns. What about rules of the household? Outlining responsibilities can help to avoid conflict later.
- What happens when an older person needs more care than the family can provide? How is this determined and what is the next step? It is best to discuss these potential scenarios before a move takes place so there are no misunderstandings later.

IS MOVING IN WITH THE KIDS RIGHT FOR YOU?

THIS IS FOR YOU IF:

- You love the idea of the kind of intergenerational living that being with kids and grandkids brings. And their friends!

- You welcome the opportunity to be a mentor to a younger generation. Often when families have been apart for years, family history gets lost. This gives all of you the time to re-connect with family traditions and history.
- You and your family have good verbal communication. This means that each party has permission to bring up even uncomfortable topics.
- You and your adult children can accept that some roles may reverse. For example, you may have to give up driving and allow your adult child or grandchild to determine when they are available to drive you places. If you become unable to cook, will you be OK with eating the vegan diet that your daughter's family prefers? These are subtle ways that choice and decision making for an older adult can erode. But these changes in self direction may be preferable to living in an assisted living.

STAY CLEAR IF:

- You and your adult children have a history of conflict that has not been resolved. Living together brings up a lot of old issues. If you do not have the experience of working things out, this could lead to much unhappiness.
- You and your family cannot talk about money. We knew one older couple who had the funds to buy a unit of a duplex apartment. They were happy that their recently divorced daughter and her school age child were going to move in with them. Unfortunately, the daughter expected the parents to put the apartment in her name even though she was not paying for it. When the parents balked, a huge conflict ensued. Now the parents have lived happily and independently in the apartment for five years. The daughter rarely makes contact.

5

NEW FRONTIERS IN SENIOR HOUSING

Priorities are changing and there is no one size fits all. As we look around and explore where and how boomers are living, we see a new frontier. The traditional choices are being joined by new ideas that may not have existed five years ago. We also wonder how some of these new offerings will meet the needs of the full life cycle.

For those still in their active years, some time-honored senior communities still hold strong. Some people love the idea of Margaritaville and Sun City. Both Margaritaville and Sun City are 55 plus communities with oodles of amenities and activities. These are self-contained communities where residents have their own houses and a community that caters to every leisure need. There are golf courses, pickleball courts, swimming pools, bars, restaurants and much more. The emphasis is on an "active" lifestyle and in the case of the Jimmy Buffet inspired Margaritaville, "the party never stops!"

This sounds fun on the surface. But, is it a type of social isolation? This type of community holds fast to the concept that older adults don't want to be bothered with young neighbors. It also buys into the attitude that younger people don't want to be reminded of old folks. It assumes that everyone will be more comfortable with age segregation.

People are showing signs of a little creativity in their retirement plans. We have seen reports of elders choosing to live places that typically would be for the short term. For example, a viral story on the internet featured a man in his mid-60's announcing his plan to move to a Holiday Inn for his retirement.[18] He researched the costs with a long term stay discount at the hotel. He figured that he could move from one long term Holiday Inn stay to another. He combined that with the senior discount and came up with the cost of about $60 a night. He compared this with the cost of the average nursing home, which is $188 a night or more. Of course, a healthy aging person does not actually need or want to live in a nursing home. And, the Holiday Inn can be a great choice for a vacation stay, but it does not offer a senior adult with added needs the kinds of personal care services that a nursing home does. But, it does not prevent an older person from interacting with younger people.

Another enterprising retiree, Lee Watchstetter, decided to make a bold move after the death of her husband left her alone and responsible for their large family home. She sold the house and moved onto a luxury cruise ship...permanently. The cost of this runs somewhat higher than the Holiday Inn or a traditional senior assisted living, but still lower than the nursing home. Ms. Watchstetter is 89 years old and has been living this lifestyle for over 12 years. She has even written a book about her retirement choice, I May Be Homeless, But You Should See My Yacht.[19]

Consider the benefits of living on a cruise ship, pre-COVID. There are always new people to meet and social and fun activities to engage you. You can explore the world, getting to know different cultures and countries, or stay in your cabin. The food, of course, is plentiful. There is nightlife and entertainment. And, all of this with onboard healthcare. Cruise lines have live-aboard doctors and nurses. Not even a nursing home has that much medical access. Granted, they will not manage chronic illnesses or significant urgent care, but for the most healthy senior, the care fills a need nicely. It is no wonder that the cruise ship industry is developing permanent residency cabins for those who want to live the sailing life year-round. Will this industry be able to pivot to satisfy the health and safety needs of the post-COVID world? We shall see. As for Ms. Watchstetter, she is reportedly living safely on land in Florida, close to family during the pandemic.[20]

Clearly, older adults are no longer interested in simply moving into the local assisted living or retirement community. The senior housing industry is scrambling to keep up with the changes. There is a desire to live the last years with a spirit of adventure. We will consider the possibilities in this chapter.

MOVING BACK TO THE CITY

As we mentioned in a previous chapter, seniors are choosing in large numbers to rent rather than own. As they shed the big house in the suburbs, older folks can choose to find smaller accommodations in their familiar neighborhoods. Or, they may choose something that harkens back to their earlier lives.

City living provides energy, opportunities, and diversity. For some, moving back to the city can make a lot of sense. The idea of being integrated, rather than segregated according to age, has appeal for some older adults.

AN ACTIVE AGING LIFE IN THE CITY OF BROTHERLY LOVE

For some, moving is familiar and therefore not intimidating. Corrine and Jack moved about 10 times in their first 20 years of marriage. They have lived in other countries as well as different states. We can learn from these role models that moving is a process that has a beginning, a middle and an end. As Corrine told us, "Once you make the decision, once you say 'Yes,' then it gets exciting." Here is their story, which involves three of their most recent moves.

While raising their two daughters, Corrine and Jack lived in Detroit, Michigan for about 15 years. They also owned a second, smaller home in Chautauqua, New York. In Chautauqua, they enjoyed summer vacations, their daughters went to summer camp, and many happy family memories were created there.

Several factors combined to push the couple to move east. After their daughters had grown into young adults and lived on their own, Corrine and Jack started to spend more time in Chautauqua. Both sets of their parents were in east coast cities. They wanted to be closer to them. Corrine found a job in Chautauqua. Jack was working remotely and could live anywhere. They made the decision that it would become their permanent home.

After a number of years of living there, the couple began to talk about their wish to live in a city. Corrine was 60 years old and her husband was 62. Chatauqua is a lovely place and on a beautiful lake, but it is a small town. They began to consider their options. Boston, Philadelphia, and New York City were on their list. The discussions narrowed to Philly and they took one trip to look at rentals there. Corrine says with a laugh, "even the rental agent didn't believe we were actually going to do it." They made their decision and began the process.

They had bought and sold many properties moving around the country and around the world. They knew the drill. They knew what to expect. When they decided to move to an apartment in Philadelphia, they were still in the process of selling their home in Michigan. The market was not good at the time and they had to sell the house at a loss. Going through each object in the home, Corrine states "it was a huge reckoning for me and my husband because we had to agree on what to let go of." They made difficult choices. "I had to let go of my grandmother's dining set. We agreed to keep artwork that we had collected together." They separated things into what to keep, what to donate, and what to sell. Then they hired an estate sale agent to manage the remaining property.

Now they live in the heart of Philadelphia, in a two-bedroom, two-bathroom apartment that is approximately 1600 square feet. They are on the 19th floor of their pet-friendly building, which features a green space between buildings of the complex. There is a gym and meeting rooms. There are lots of young people as well as retirees. There are some families with young children. Corrine loves this combination of ages. They are friendly with people in the building. In terms of making new friends, however, they have found more connections with people that they meet at museum events and activities out of the building.

Their lifestyle is well suited for this urban hub. In addition to many museums and art galleries, there is also a vibrant walking path along the river. Restaurants and shops are easily accessible. Jack and Corrine estimate that they walk about seven miles a day. In fact, while we were conducting this interview, Corrine was walking at a fast pace to her next activity! She volunteers at a local hospital twice a week as a baby cuddler in the NICU. It's two miles of walking each way. She loves that this move keeps her physically fit.

We asked if there were any regrets about the move to the two-bedroom rental apartment. Jack says "space." They can't grill at their building and he is a terrific cook. In New York state, they had an herb garden and enjoyed tending to their yard themselves. They miss this. When they think about the future, they really don't think about buying property again. "When there is a problem in a rental, it's so much easier to call the super to fix it." Corrine can see them moving again if and when their daughters have families of their own. Corrine would love to be close to grandchildren. She and Jack joke about where they will live next. One daughter is recently engaged. She and her future husband may go to Boston where he grew up. Corrine and Jack would love to live in Boston so that may be the next place of their future.

WHAT HAPPENED TO CORRINE AND JACK AFTER COVID HIT?

Are you still happy to live in the smaller square footage?
Yes, we are still happy to live here. We even had the addition of one of our adult daughters come to live with us for 10 weeks during her initial remote work period. The space worked out very comfortably for all of us, from a professional and personal standpoint. We are fortunate to have two bathrooms and a second bedroom set up as a den with a pull out couch, which helped us all feel like we had enough space together. We also have a balcony and a relatively large amount of green space both in our complex and nearby, so we don't feel at all confined or cramped.

Are you still glad to be in the urban setting? What has it been like for you there?
Yes, we are still glad to be in our urban setting. Being in a city with excellent health care systems is more important to us than ever, given the pandemic. The city's location relative to where our other family members live, primarily here and along the east coast, remains a big plus. Philadelphia has its share of troubles and challenges. However, we feel informed and aware in ways that allow us to live here safely and enjoyably.

An extremely smart thing the city of Philadelphia did in mid-March was to close down a 5 mile stretch of Martin Luther King Drive from the art museum to the East Falls Bridge to vehicular traffic completely. This allows people to bicycle, run, and walk 24/7. This encourages outdoor activity, alleviates some of the crowding on the popular Schuylkill River Trail, and enables better social distancing. We use it pretty much every single day.

Any other thoughts you might want to add to share with our readers?
We are fortunate to continue to have our family vacation home in a non-urban setting. This allows us and other family members to "get away" from the city, when desired, and enjoy a more rural setting. This allows us to enjoy our urban setting all the more.

ARE YOU READY TO LIVE IN A MICRO-APARTMENT?

In large urban areas, the lack of affordable housing has become a national issue. In response, rental companies have created dormitory-style housing that provides tiny private spaces mixed with large community spaces. They may offer a private room, a shared room, even a bunk bed! For young people who are just a few years out of college, this communal living close to jobs and city life may be palatable. It may not be too big a sacrifice as they are building their resumes.

What is intriguing is that some older adults are drawn to this lifestyle. As some elders move back to the city, they are looking for affordability, activities, and diversity.[21] Developers of apartments designed for people in their 30's have been surprised how popular their properties have been for retired adults. An example of this is a hip, co-living start-up company called Ollie. They have sites in a number of large east coast cities. These buildings offer rentals of "micro-apartments" with hotel-style, "all-inclusive" amenities. Those amenities include maid service, linens, social gatherings in the building and in nearby venues. They even have a social club membership with some leases. The locations offer an urban neighborhood and a wide array of accessible arts, restaurants, and nightlife. To active boomers ditching the large suburban house and responsibilities, the appeal is clear.

A FAMILY MOVES TO OLLIE

For Jim and his wife Nancy, their move to Ollie started with some bad news. Nancy had a job that she loved in the city. She commuted to and from their home in the suburbs of New Jersey. Unfortunately, her company started laying off positions, including her own. Jim, who had also spent most of his career taking the daily train to the city for work from their lovely suburban home, had retired a few years earlier. They had raised their children in their spacious, 5,000 square foot house. They enjoyed their garden and yard immensely. When Nancy's father passed away five years ago, they invited her mother, Kay, then in her 80s, to move in with them.

The layoff took all of them by surprise. It resulted in many discussions and thoughts about what they wanted to do next. Suddenly, many new possibilities were on the table. They had both gone to college in the Pittsburgh area and loved it there. They still had friends and some relatives there. They knew that they wanted to continue to have city amenities and an urban lifestyle. They began to research on the web and found the Ollie development. It piqued their interest. "We realized that we did not want to stay in the suburbs. Pittsburgh offers mental stimulation and a community close to colleges. Oh! And we had just adopted a puppy. So, we knew we had to find a place in the city that would accommodate a puppy, our older dog, my wife and myself and my mother-in-law."

Before they knew it, a plan was forming. They did not even go to look at the property in person. They toured the two-bedroom apartment by FaceTime. The rental agent made sure to show them the generous dog park nearby. They signed the lease online. Then things got really busy.

Jim describes that in a six week period of time, they put their home of 36 years on the market, had multiple yard sales and gave away belongings to friends as quickly as possible. When asked what it was like to do this rapid downsizing, Jim laughs. "As a friend of mine said, it's like ripping off a Band-Aid! Don't look back or you will turn to stone." He said that as hard as it was for him and his wife, downsizing was even harder on his 85-year-old mother-in-law. Still grieving from the loss of her husband and a World War II refugee, Kay had experienced multiple losses in her life. Her possessions had so much meaning for her. "She understood that she had the option of living elsewhere, but knew that she wanted to continue to live with us. So she made the difficult choice of letting things go." The house sold within six weeks, and off they went to Pittsburgh.

The family of three people and two dogs have lived at Ollie for almost a year. After a month or so, they moved from a two-bedroom, 717 square foot apartment to a three-bedroom, 1500 square feet apartment in the building. Both Jim and Nancy are quite happy that they made this choice and this move. They are also fortunate that they have had a family vacation cabin in the mountains for many years. They know that if they feel closed in, they can take off to enjoy some wilderness and space.

At first, they asked themselves "Are we going to fit in?" But they have found that it has not been awkward. Yes, they are older on the continuum of residents at Ollie. However, they have enjoyed what they see as benefits of being in a more diverse community than the New Jersey suburbs. Jim enjoys their neighbors who are transplants from different parts of the world and who are a variety of ages and professions. Ollie has monthly social gatherings and he and Nancy have made friends there. He admits that for his mother-in-law, the transition has been harder. Kay is healthy and mobile, goes to the grocery store now and then, but other than that, stays mostly in the apartment.

When asked about the future, Jim says that they have just signed an additional two-year lease. "I wouldn't be surprised if we do that again at the end of this lease." They haven't really given a lot of thought further than that. Their adult children live in different states. Jim does not foresee living with either of them in the way that his mother-in-law resides with him and his wife. The location suits them well. There are top-notch hospitals and clinics within walking distance. Jim and Nancy have long-term care insurance if needed. Currently, they are both fit and healthy. As a matter of fact, his wife's job contacted her after they moved and re-hired her. This time she's working remotely from home. Nancy is very happy with this arrangement.

Any regrets? "We miss the garden a little bit."

WHAT HAPPENED TO JIM AND NANCY AND KAY WHEN COVID HIT?

Are you still glad to be in the urban setting? What has it been like for you there since COVID started?
We are unique in that we have two places we live at. For the last two and half months we have been at our cabin in the Adirondacks. We recently have come back to Pittsburgh for a couple of weeks to gather things and reconnect.

In the Adirondacks we had physical space but were socially distant. At Ollie, we have social connections but we are physically limited. Being back in Pittsburgh we have rediscovered all the joys that make urban life great. Diverse restaurants, the ability to walk pretty much everywhere for all our needs. Our infrastructure is better in terms of internet here than at our cabin. There, we rely a lot on wireless internet access (for Nancy's remote work). In the Adirondacks, we were totally surrounded by nature. We felt we were distant from the scenes of chaos and life in the COVID world. Surrounded by the forest we were able to disconnect. We subtly participated in what the Japanese call forest bathing, or shinrin yoku. The ability to reconnect with nature. Over time that gets limiting, and there is a yearning for social connections.

How is your mother-in-law, Kay, doing? Has she gone back and forth with you and your wife during this time? Does she have a preference between the two settings?
Yes, my mother-in-law has gone back and forth with us. She didn't really want to leave, she thought that there is no one up there to interact with. In reality, there is some social interaction. We got together (with neighbors there) for dinner. My mother-in-law actually came out of her shell and was very interactive. My wife and I noted it, and realized the role of social interactions have as we get older.

At first, when we got there in early March, Kay was a little gloomy.

At the time it was still the last gasps of winter. Over time, she has come to like it. One of the main things was that we started a vegetable garden up there, and she is anxious to see that. I think she likes the urban setting, but with COVID, it probably restricts her more.

If you had not had the escape hatch (the cabin) that you have, what would your thoughts be about social distancing in the urban setting?
Social distancing in an urban setting can be frustrating. You are surrounded by all these people, but it seems like virtual settings are the norm. Zoom cocktail hours and Zoom classes are good substitutes, but seem to be less than 100% satisfaction. We do take advantage of the parks here since we have two golden retrievers that need lots of daily exercise. I think with everyone being in the same boat with the limitations makes it somewhat tolerable.

A LIFE TRANSITION AT 53 LEADS TO A MOVE TO OLLIE

Hector has lived a classic, adult New Yorker life. He lived for 20 years in Westchester County and commuted by train and by bus to his job in Manhattan. Hector and his mother lived in a two-bedroom rental home with a yard. The commute was two hours each day. As the years went by, he became wearier of the time lost and the cost of transportation.

Hector's mother passed away in 2012. With his loss and sadness came thoughts and questions about where he was living. Did he want to continue to live in Westchester? Did he want to continue his daily, grinding commute? "I realized at that time that I wanted to make my life more efficient."

He began the search for a place to live in the city. He discovered Ollie and wondered if he could manage to live in a micro-apartment. The more he thought about it the more he realized that he could do it. "I just thought I could learn to be organized." When Hector toured the Ollie micro-apartments, it was an option to choose an unfurnished studio. (Now, most of these studios come furnished and feature a Murphy bed.) At that time, Hector decided to bring a sleeper couch.

However, he soon learned that the downsizing process was

formidable. "It was a nightmare!" Hector's mother had filled the attic from top to bottom with belongings and clutter. That was a big job. He had to decide what he could bring with him and what he could not. He knew that he wanted to bring his own china and some cooking supplies. He knew that he wanted a chandelier from the home that he had lived in. He gave many things away to friends.

Finally, he moved to his micro-apartment with 40 boxes into an approximately 250 square feet unit. It was a challenge to figure out where to put everything. "It was like a puzzle!" He had to purchase a table small enough to fit, and 4 chairs. He also invested in a storage ottoman on wheels that has been very handy in his small space.

Hector is now 55 years old. He has lived at Ollie for one and a half years. "It is like heaven on earth." His apartment is on the second floor of a nine-story building. He made sure to choose a unit that has a huge beautiful window facing the park. A niece assisted with decorating the small space. "I brought my history with me, I have a few curios and many family photos on the wall." The building is on a cul-de-sac which makes it a quieter choice in the city. He has declined the optional light cleaning service at this time because he does it well himself. He loves the roof terrace that features a grill for residents. Hector has gotten so used to his sleeper sofa, that when he traveled recently and slept in a real bed, he couldn't get to sleep!

Hector recognizes that he has made some lifestyle changes as a result of his decision to live in a micro-apartment. "I definitely don't shop the way I used to." He has even noticed that this affects his food choices. "In the city, if I need a pepper or an onion for making dinner that night, I just pick it up at the bodega on the way home from work. I don't need that much. I don't have a lot of food going to waste anymore."

Hector says that neighbors enjoy the organized get-togethers once a month. "I noticed that the older residents don't participate as much, I try to invite them personally." Hector has enjoyed the common spaces and has even been able to use them for entertaining work clients. As a travel professional, Hector invited the Honduran Consult for a wine and cheese reception in one of the beautiful rooms of the building. It was a great success.

Asked about his plans for retirement, Hector pauses. He

emphasizes, "IF I retire, I want to continue to live here. Maybe at that time, I will need a little more help. Then I will choose to have light housekeeping. And, I will certainly get a Murphy bed." He loves living in this building that has in-house supervision and security, and clean and stylish common areas. He loves that he is minutes from work and all that the city has to offer. He even has an inflatable mattress for when nieces or nephews come to visit and stay overnight. And he still goes back to Westchester on the weekends to visit family.

TINY HOUSES AND ACCESSORY DWELLING UNITS

We are sure you have heard about the tiny house movement. But what is it exactly? "The tiny-house movement (also known as the "small-house movement"[22]) is an architectural and social movement that advocates living simply in small homes."

What does this have to do with aging? Well, suppose you want to downsize, but believe that renting is a bad choice financially. You worked hard to buy and own a home. You want to continue to own something that has value. You could at least leave some property to your spouse or children. The idea of renting and letting a landlord make decisions about the property feels like a backward move.

There are home-ownership choices. Some people prefer to downsize considerably and opt for a tiny house that has aging in place design features built-in.[23] In other cases, depending upon zoning laws, tiny houses that are referred to as "accessory dwelling units" can be built on the same lot as an existing home. That way someone can be close (very close!) to a family member while having their own private home to retreat to.

Construction companies across the country are now specializing in designing and pre-fabricating these small homes. They are small, but are designed with efficiency. The accessory dwelling units generally include small kitchens, a full bath, a bedroom and living space. Because they are largely pre-built and delivered to the property to be installed, they are more affordable than building from the ground up. Some areas even allow the unit to be a rental, so that families have the option to earn income on their investment. Zoning laws vary widely across the country and even county to county.

CONDOMINIUMS

Condominiums can be a viable alternative or "step down" from single-family home ownership.

The advantage of a condominium is the lack of lawn care and other maintenance tasks. Most condominium buildings have elevators and covered parking. But, buyer beware. Most condominiums have homeowners associations and homeowners fees, which can be substantial. And these fees can rise every year. Some associations do not allow someone to move out and rent their condominium to someone else.

We interviewed Susan who sold her house to move into a condominium, due to unexpected and unforeseen circumstances. It is human nature to accept the status quo, but Susan's story is a good example of why planning ahead can avoid stress later.

SUSAN'S STORY

I work full time and plan to for another couple of years even though I am 70 years old. I like working. I had a home and I sold it after my partner died. My partner handled all of the finances and there was quite a bit I didn't know about. I found out in a hurry though. When we were together, I just went along and didn't get involved at all. It was incredibly stressful to deal with not only the loss but all the details I didn't know about. I want to avoid that in the future. I want to be more responsible and accountable.

I could move out of state and work full time and be nearer my sister, but I have friends and community here. I live in a condo that I bought a year ago and I like being centrally located downtown and near the University. I have talked with my friends about buying a condo here and then purchasing one for a caregiver to live in later when we need one. That is my ideal plan. But no one has done it. I keep trying to recruit people to move here. Most people don't think about aging at all. Or they don't have the financial resources. They aren't willing to sell their houses yet.

I have three friends that already live in my condo complex and that is the reason I chose this place. I wanted a place that had all the elements of a house without the maintenance issues. There is no snow removal or lawn care. I need to have a social environment and this provides that. I run into people every day. Since suddenly losing my partner three years ago I am much more aware of the need to plan ahead and not wait for a crisis.

I have a history of working in long term care and I saw all of the older people who had children that didn't take care of them. I don't have children, and I am concerned about who will take care of me. So, it's not as if having children guarantees that they will be there for you, but I still think about it. I am starting to think about things before I need it, something I never did before.

SENIOR RESIDENCES ON COLLEGE CAMPUSES

Developing senior residences on college campuses (referred to as University-Based Retirement Communities or UBRCs) is an idea whose time has come. The reasons are varied, but economics is certainly one of them. With declining state support for colleges and universities and ample available land, the opportunity is ripe for a win-win situation. Colleges have an additional revenue stream and seniors can take classes and mingle with a younger generation.

This idea is not a pipe dream. There are already over 100 UBRCs across the country.[24] Some are smaller homes, others are condos and some are high rise apartment buildings. The appeal to seniors is obvious – opportunities for mentoring, lectures, access to campus amenities, and the excitement of being around diverse young people.

Although the idea sounds perfect for some, buy-in and monthly fees can be stiff.[25] By stiff, we mean over a million for buy-in and up to $9000 a month on top of that. Not all students are enthusiastic about the idea, however. Some have expressed concerns about how noise will affect older residents. Add to that, the notion that young people want to get away from their parents and grandparents when they go off to college, not live with them.

MULTI AND INTERGENERATIONAL USE

The topic of housing in the United States has become a significant and complicated issue. Affordability and accessibility are the same for Millennials as for the older generation. Moreover, adult children want their parents closer to where they live. Younger generations gravitate to urban areas for the same reasons along with increased employment opportunities or colleges.

You can see where we are going with this... multi-generational housing is a logical solution to many of these problems. And developers are taking notice. Using existing housing stock in cities to develop intergenerational use makes sense. Another trend is to incorporate housing into buildings that have been mostly commercial real estate. First, let's look at the definition of multi-use and intergenerational use.

MULTI-USE

Multi-use refers to developments that incorporate housing including everything from restaurants, retail and healthcare to luxury hotels and/or student housing. This alleviates assisted living communities from having to provide every amenity for their residents. Multi-use also allows for greater opportunities for partnerships. Many seniors these days want choices. They want many restaurants to choose from, not just the one typically available in senior housing. Walkability is another desired commodity. For active and able seniors, being able to walk to stores, and even healthcare is a bonus.

The Clean Slate Project is a recently released report by the architectural firm Perkins Eastman. They examine trends in housing and communities that influence the lives of seniors and where they will live. One concept that stands out is that of the Vertical Main Street.[26] This entails an urban setting with a single building that includes senior living homes, retail space, and community use such as childcare.

While this idea may partly still be on the drawing board, there are existing homes for seniors in the US and abroad in these multi-use buildings. For example, St. Paul's Towers in Oakland, California, is a complete senior living community in a multi-use building in Adams

Point and overlooking Lake Merritt. The studio to 2 bedroom apartments includes independent living, assisted living and more health care options available. The facility itself includes events, classes and social gatherings. There is a rooftop terrace and a state of the art gym. Residents can interact with the commercial occupants of the building and neighborhood. Multiple businesses and offices exist on the storefront level which provides convenience and interest for senior residents.

INTERGENERATIONAL OR MULTI-GENERATIONAL HOUSING

Intergenerational housing is the blending of families with school-age children, young adults and seniors living together in the same housing community. The concept may include cohousing with separate living quarters, high rise apartments, or homesharing with different generations. This type of housing is gaining in popularity for a variety of reasons. Some are economic and others are social.

- Living with people of differing ages is viewed as being a positive and energizing experience. This provides an opportunity for people to come together as a community and to learn and grow. Seniors who live in multigenerational housing describe how interesting and exciting this environment is.
- More and more families are becoming intergenerational based on necessity. An older adult moves in with a child or a college-age child moves back in with the parents. Having other housing options available can help families maintain the family unit. According to the Pew Research Center, a record 64 million Americans live in multigenerational households. This is defined as including two or more adult generations, including grandparents and grandchildren younger than 25 years old.
- Segregating people by age does not make economic sense. If people of different ages want to live together, they should have that opportunity. Seniors still have lots of age-restricted options if they choose.

LESLIE'S GRANDPARENTS' HOME –
THREE HOMES UNDER ONE ROOF

From an early age, Leslie was exposed to an elder group living situation that was multi-generational.

After World War II, her grandparents were almost finished raising their four children. With two siblings, they scraped enough money together to build their own home. Her grandfather designed the house. The largest part of the house was a family-sized home that had three bedrooms. It led to a porch on the main level. The porch connected to a tiny, single floor apartment. This apartment had two bedrooms, one bathroom, a living space with room for a breakfast nook and a minuscule kitchen. This apartment was shared by Leslie's grandmother's unmarried sister and her unmarried brother. On the basement level was a one-car garage and another small apartment with its own entrance. That apartment was always rented to a college student.

Over time, the four children grew up and married and moved away. The grandparents, great aunt, and great uncle and the college student(s) remained. By then, there were lots of grandchildren. The home (except for the college student apartment) became a default child care center. Leslie remembers being there with her siblings and cousins regularly. "As kids, we spent countless hours there. We enjoyed playing in the spacious yard. Some helped in my grandmother's vegetable and flower gardens. My grandfather constructed a tree swing for us and built a large sandbox surrounded by cinder blocks in which he carved each grandchild's name. There were rocking chairs on the porch, and we would sit there in the warmer months with our elders. We shucked peas, heard family stories and gossip with lots of chuckling."

Inside, her grandmother and great aunt canned peaches and tomatoes and lined the pantry shelves with the jars. Her grandmother taught the girls how to sew on her old push pedal Singer sewing machine.

Her grandfather passed away. Her great uncle continued to work at his business into his eighties. He drove a Mustang, was increasingly deaf, and gave the grandchildren rides to swimming lessons in the summer. The grandkids suffered through many hours of watching the Lawrence Welk Show with their elders.

Eventually, the grandchildren went off to college and their own adult lives. All three of the elders in the house remained. Now in their eighties and beyond, they slowly declined. Leslie's great uncle sold his business and soon after, he developed dementia. In about a year, he had died. Her grandmother also became (as it was referred to at the time) "senile." Her father's sister, who lived nearby, took care of the grandmother while she remained at home with the help of some home aides as long as possible. After that, Leslie's grandmother spent a brief time in a nursing home before she passed away. Finally, her great aunt was the only one in residence. Though she still had her wits about her, she developed diabetes. After a leg amputation, she lived her last two years in a nursing home until her death at age 96.

Leslie had a special affinity for that house. She would love to live in a similar design for her own advanced years. Her grandfather's creation did not have the benefit of the modern universal design features of to-day. However, it allowed aging people to have mobility and access. First, there were three unique units. Each unit varied in size, permitting mul-tigenerational use under one roof. Each unit had privacy but was ac-cessible to the others. There were full bathrooms on each unit's main floor. There was plenty of natural light and ease of seeing the outdoors from inside. There was a comfortable and accessible outdoor space on the porch with a view of the green landscape. Each unit had an entrance to the street without stairs. And, there was a legal apartment to provide some revenue and a bit of interaction with a college-aged person. All in a house that would be considered tiny by today's standards. And even without raised toilets, roll-in showers or widened doorways, its inhabit-ants lived there until they were in their late 80's and their 90's.

THE NEW FRONTIER OF SENIOR HOUSING OPTIONS: PROS AND CONS

PROS:

- Trying something new can be a great adventure and provide an opportunity to meet new people and live in an unfamiliar setting.
- If choosing a rental, an older adult may decide in advance that

it will be a short term plan. For example, you could choose to live an exciting few years in New York City, go to plays and art museums. This could be a lifelong dream come true...with an expiration date. Then, you could move again and settle closer to children and grandchildren in a more traditional senior living situation.

- Some options may be less expensive than owning and living in a large single-family home.

CONS:

- Becoming a renter after years of being a homeowner could be difficult. Think of the control that a landlord or leasing agency would have. What if the rent increases? What if needed repairs go unserviced? What if the owner decides to sell the property? There can be some concerns and hassles being a tenant.
- Not all of the new living options discussed in this chapter are available in all parts of the country or in smaller markets.
- Multi-use buildings that offer senior communities may be costly for most. There may be some that exist that have private apartments or condominiums, but do not include assistive services.
- Evaluate costs of any these options you are considering since they could be too high to be sustainable over the long run.

SHOULD YOU TRY LIVING IN A
NEW FRONTIER HOME?

THIS IS RIGHT FOR YOU IF:

- You love trying something new and different.
- You're bored with your present living situation and want to be in a new environment. An unusual 80-year-old we know hates anything old. She doesn't like old furniture. She doesn't like to live where other people have lived before her. She loves new construction and design.

- You are flexible and are ready to deal with some unexpected issues.
- You welcome being in closer proximity to other people, either in your home or your building.

STAY CLEAR IF:

- You are risk-averse and don't like change. Many of these new housing options require flexibility and a sense of adventure. You may not like that, and that's ok! It may not be the right time for going out of your comfort zone.
- Intergenerational living sounds like being back with your kids! The noise, the occasional chaos are more than you want to bargain for.
- You don't like the responsibility and pressure of being a landlord or landlady.
- Cost is an issue. Some of these options may save money in the end. Others will require more investment than you feel comfortable with.

6

EXPATS: LIVING THE DREAM RETIREMENT IN ANOTHER COUNTRY

Why on earth would someone of retirement age decide to move away from family and friends to a country abroad? The biggest answers: finances and a sense of adventure. In the countries that people are moving to, the out of pocket costs that Medicare doesn't cover in the states can be significantly lower in other countries. Not to mention that living costs overall are lower. In some countries, US citizens can opt into the country's healthcare system while maintaining their Medicare for trips back to the states. Property and labor costs are also lower. The nest eggs that people have built over decades that might not last a person's lifetime in the US will stretch much further abroad.

How many Americans live abroad? There is no way of knowing exactly, but we can get an idea from the social security administration. It reports[27] that in 2016 social security checks are sent to about a half-million Americans living abroad. Some people live part-time abroad and visit the states to see friends and family.

WHY PEOPLE MAKE THE CHOICE TO LIVE ABROAD

- For many people, living abroad fulfills a lifelong dream of adventure and exploration. It also allows them to do so at an affordable cost. For empty nesters who are in good health, moving to another country is an exciting journey.

- Healthcare costs for seniors are soaring. It is not unusual these days for seniors to go to other countries for surgeries that are a fraction of the cost in the U.S. Prescription medications are also significantly lower. Why not move to a country that offers these healthcare savings?

- The weather is better. A year-round moderate climate can be a big draw. It allows for the enjoyment of activities such as water sports, hiking, tennis, and so on. Staying more active promotes better health.

- A chance to explore a new culture and learn a new language. Some people fulfill a need to contribute by volunteering in another country. Others simply want to immerse themselves in a completely new experience.

HARRY AND SALLY'S STORY

We talked to Harry, 79, and Sally, 73. They are an American couple who made the big move from the US to Panama several years ago. We asked how they made their choice and what it is like to live as an expat in that country. While we can imagine the appeal of the climate and how they connected personally to their new country, some of their answers may surprise you.

Where were you living before you moved to another country? Had you already retired?
We were living on the Eastern Shore of Virginia. We had already retired.

How did you decide to make this move?
I think we made it decades ago. Long before we could. Although we've been to several Caribbean islands and to Hawaii, we had our first real tropical experience in Peru (for six weeks) in 1979. It was magical, for both of us. It took me six months to stop wanting to stow-away and go back. We had opportunities, both business and work-related, to travel to the tropics after that and always loved that when we were

there, so we began to look at those travels as possibilities for retirement. When we retired, in 2001, we moved to the Eastern Shore of Virginia and lived there for 13 years, but after our first winter there, we spent two and a half to four months each winter traveling and living in the tropics (South America, Asia, Africa, Australia). Although Sally was very happy in Virginia, I began to want a change in venue about halfway through, so the last five or six winters we were much more intentional about looking at tropical home possibilities and by the last couple of years, we were pretty committed to it.

How long did it take to move and get settled?
In January of 2014, we spent a month in Gamboa, Panama, and loved it. We did some house looking there, before going on to Trinidad and Tobago, where we decided to buy a house in Gamboa. That March we returned via Panama and closed the deal.

What are the expenses like compared to costs in the US?
Not appreciably different. Panama is first world in many respects, and our lifestyle didn't change.

Do you get health care in your adopted country? Do you have confidence in the healthcare system to meet your needs for the foreseeable future?
We do, but we have to pay for it and then file claims with our secondary health insurer because there is no Medicare coverage for people living voluntarily out of the US. The health system is tiered and the top-tier is equivalent to the US.

We had the opportunity to get the Panamanian health care early in 2014 before either of us turned 74, but we opted not to. We had Medicare with BCBS as secondary, so we decided that we didn't need local. As Emeritus Professors, we are permanently eligible for the group secondary insurance (in our retirement plan), so that plus Medicare is what we have. We do an annual medical visit to the US, where we stay with Sally's brother and wife for 3-4 weeks each fall. The medical expenses for those weeks go through Medicare. The rest of the year we are in Panama, so pay our medical expenses out of pocket and, if the expenses are very large, we file a claim with Blue Cross Blue Shield, through Blue Cross Blue Shield's international claims department.

I've had one accident (a fall) and three surgeries here (squamous cell carcinoma removal, repair of Achilles tendon tear, kidney stone removal) for which hospital involvement was necessary, and all went smoothly. I rate the medical treatment here equivalent to the US. Mind you, two of the hospitals were private and only one was public, but the service and care were equivalent at all three. However, the costs were much less at the public hospital. Blue Cross Blue Shield of Panama is available, as are several other health insurance plans. If we had been cut loose from our group plan when we retired, we would certainly have enrolled in one of those.

Were you fluent in the language of the country that you retired to?
No, and unfortunately we're still not.

What has it been like? What are the things that you enjoy most?
Moving here was, for us, like finally coming home. Before retirement we were both biology professors and living in Gamboa is very much like living in a university community – very mixed culturally, with lots of well-educated and professional people, foreigners and Panamanians. The Smithsonian Tropical Research Center headquarters are in Panama, and Gamboa is a major site. It is situated at the end of the road and inside Soberania National Park, so it is surrounded on three sides by tropical forest and by the Panama Canal on the fourth. The houses are built around green zones that are continuous with the forest, so we have a plethora of jungle animals and plants in our yards. There is no commerce here, so we have to drive to Panama City for amenities and supplies, but that is only a 20 to 30-minute drive away, much of which is through a lovely tropical forest. We love the climate. Daily highs are around 86 degrees Fahrenheit, overnight lows around 75 degrees Fahrenheit. All year-round. Being biologists we love the abundance of plants and animals. We also love the tranquility.

What have the challenges of living in another culture been for you? What surprised you most, good and bad, about moving to another country?
Language is our biggest, and perhaps only challenge. We had lived for extensive periods in foreign countries and were very experienced travelers by the time we moved here, so Panama was a breeze for us.

Gamboa is the former Canal Zone, which was US territory for almost a century, so the cultural differences were minimal.

What would you advise someone nearing retirement age in the US who is considering this option?
Take intensive language lessons for a long time (years, if possible) before you move. Spend several continuous months, or even a year or two, living where you think you want to move before you burn bridges. Living in a foreign country is living, dealing with all the usual chores and hassles. It is not a vacation. Plan to spend twice as much time doing many things than you are used to.

How often, if at all, do you come back to visit the states?
Once a year, for two or three weeks, to visit friends and to maintain US medical contacts in case we have to move back.

Do you plan on staying in your adopted country for the rest of your life or is there a point at which you would consider a move back to the states?
At this point, Panama is our home. We plan to stay here until we die.

Any regrets?
None.

WHAT HAPPENED TO HARRY AND SALLY WHEN COVID HIT?

Unfortunately, the first month of the shutdown in Panama was scary for Harry and Sally. Their home was burglarized and cash was stolen. Other neighbors' homes were also broken into. Harry reports that "The village went on high-alert for a while and the police upped their patrols a bit. After that, there were no more incidents." Here, Harry answers more of our questions:

What has it been like for you to adjust to shelter-in-place orders or restrictions in your community?
We have led a rather isolated and solitary lifestyle together for decades, so we had almost no adjustments to make. Sally has two,

hour-long Zoom sessions per week with her yoga guru and does a bit of that on her own on the other days. The biggest (adjustment) was having to give up national and international travels, but even that wasn't a hardship.

Initially, we laid in a large enough supply of food, drinks, fuel and funds for two months. Except for the money theft, that all went well. Gamboa is a rather isolated community. It was totally lacking in commercial amenities and surrounded by tropical forest in a national park. We had not anticipated that delivery services and local amenities would emerge as a result of the quarantine, but they have. We used to make at least two, full-day trips into Panama City per week. Now we only make two, two-hour trips per month.

In truth, for us it has actually become easier and more pleasant to live here now than before the contagion. We are old, retired and used to entertaining ourselves and being alone together. The quarantine has made so many activities forbidden that there is much less noise and much less traffic. So things are much more tranquil. And there is less air & water pollution. We realize, of course, that the epidemic is horrible and a curse. We are not fans!

Do these restrictions result in you feeling more isolated?
No.

Do you feel confident about your access to health care should you get COVID?
Confident, no. Hopeful, yes. So far, Panama has managed to contain the level of infections. However, that could – and may – happen tomorrow.

Have you reconsidered your choice to live there?
Absolutely not!

Any other thoughts about COVID and your future?
We fervently hope that our future is COVIDLESS. We hope that a vaccine will be developed against it. We hope that this disastrous experience will at least be informative and lead to better ways to prevent and deal with future such outbreaks.

HOW A MOVE ABROAD IMPACTS FAMILY: THREE GENERATIONS AND A MOVE TO COSTA RICA

While many may daydream about a life in the tropics, some issues may prevent the fantasy from going further. A primary sticking point will be "What about my family? How can I leave them?"

But, what if the family is part of the motivation for making the choice to move to another country? Below, we will hear the story of Estelle, as told after her death by her son Ben.

Estelle and Ben's father had been divorced for many years and she lived and worked as a social worker throughout her career in New York City. She had focused her work life on the care of children and families. Estelle had experienced bouts of depression throughout her life as well as alcoholism. "My mother had become involuntarily re-tired in her fifties. She moved from NYC to Palo Alto, California to live with her mother who was starting to have dementia."

But this move was not an easy one for Estelle. She couldn't find adequate work in Palo Alto and started commuting to San Francisco. "She hated the Palo Alto cold. She hated any cold, anything less than about 75F. Her mother was starting to need care 24 hours a day, as she was pretty demented and would wake up at strange hours and occasionally wander, get disoriented and not know how to get back home. There was basically nothing in the way of treatment at that time and it was more than my mother could do on her own." The only real assets that the elderly mother and now retired daughter had was the mother's house. "After talking with her brother and possibly her mother, it was decided my mother and grandmother would sell the house and relocate someplace warm." They also needed to move to a country where elderly care and help were affordable. "While in Palo Alto, my mother had gone to Mexico a few times and maybe Panama and she did go to Costa Rica." They chose Costa Rica.

Soon, Estelle and her mother had made the move. "It was quick. She moved, found a place to rent, found help and established herself pretty quickly. She moved from place to place a couple of times but given how long she lived there I thought it was pretty stable. She did not speak Spanish and didn't pick it up easily or quickly but she made do."

"She moved to San Jose, the capital and rented a reasonable apartment in an OK neighborhood. Not an expat ghetto. Rent and other expenses were cheap, much cheaper than Palo Alto would have been. Food was not much cheaper – local veggies were, but meat and dairy not really. Also, she had good luck finding people who really cared and were nice to my grandmother." Some of the caregivers lived in, and for that the cost was even less.

We asked Ben about his mother's and grandmother's health care in Costa Rica. "Yes. She got good health care there. For my grandmother, there really wasn't anything medically they could do/give her, but they did take care of her. Later, when I went down and went to my mother's doctor with her, he spent 45 minutes with us on her appointment. He spoke perfect English and, I was told, German (he had a German name but was born in Costa Rica). I think for standard medical problems, Costa Rica's hospitals and private health insurance clinics were as good as typical care in the US. If you needed micro brain surgery, likely not. But there are lots of old people with typical old people problems and they seemed to do a very good job of taking care of them."

For Estelle, the move to this country opened up experiences for her. While she didn't speak the language well, she didn't let it stop her. "In tourist areas, English was spoken and she quickly learned enough or had a pocket translation guide so she could make her wants known."

Ben went on to describe what Estelle's life was like and how it evolved over the years that she lived there. "While she spent a lot of time taking care of her mother for the first years, she had a great time. Costa Rica is a thin part of central America with mountains, volcanoes, and beaches. She traveled all over for a few days at a time. When she arrived (in the late 1980s), she could fly from San Jose (mountains) to a jungle airstrip by the beach for something like $9-12 on a very old DC-12 or 6. It was a four-hour drive or a twenty or thirty-minute flight much of which was taxiing before or after landing. The flights were basically daily when there were enough paying passengers. She liked traveling."

"She also volunteered at a girls' school for runaways in San Jose." Estelle had become aware of the horrifying "child sex tours" that exploited the children of Costa Rica and other tourist destinations. "After going to Costa Rica, she volunteered and worked with troubled and at-risk children. Later she catalyzed a publicity effort highlighting existing child sex tourism and, I think, had a real impact in forcing the government to be more open about the problem which in turn helped reduce it in Costa Rica."

"For much of her stay, things were very safe with almost no violent crime. Things changed later. I haven't been there in 14 years but things never got really dangerous when she was first there. Violent crime was pretty much non-existent or at least it seemed that way. Later, one would need to be careful at night in the city or alone or on country roads at night."

Estelle formed strong opinions about life in Costa Rica as an expat. Her son explains "She generally liked the locals despite having trouble communicating with them. She found most of the other US and Canadian expats spoiled and exploitative. She thought many of the US and Canadians expected the Costa Ricans to be happy to work 24/7 for slave wages. She said Mexico had much more culture and civilization, but Costa Rica was just friendlier."

After her mother passed away, Estelle continued life in Costa Rica. In the beginning, she found life there good. As time went on though, she began to experience her own health challenges. Ben describes this time of her life. "About 18 years ago, she had a psychiatric break that may have been brought on by one or more strokes and memory issues that ensued. We managed to convince her to have a friend help her get on a plane back to California. She stayed with us for a couple of months and then at an assisted living place here. But she hated the cold and she too was showing signs of dementia. We managed to hire her ex housekeeper in Costa Rica and sent her back for a trial run. It worked great for us and her. We were very lucky because we hadn't pre-organized it years before. But her housekeeper, Edi, was a really good person and was happy to take care of my mother with a little additional help. Edi invited my mother to Edi's family's parties and gatherings. Again, medically we were of the opinion that the care she got there was at least as good as she would have gotten here."

"Later my mother developed congestive heart failure with breathing problems (years of smoking) and needed more medical attention.

But again, as far as we can tell she got good to excellent care there. When she was here after the break, we had her checked out by our doctors and had some psych testing. The recommended treatment here was basically identical to what they suggested in Costa Rica."

Estelle was a complex person, who had real-life ups and downs in her new country. Ben understood that his mother was fully capable of making her own choices. At times, "she was full of regrets, but not about moving to Costa Rica. I am sure she was lonely at first and even later on, but, especially when she first moved there and was in good health, she thought she was living a queen's life. Traveling to the beach, then going to a "resort" by one of the volcanoes. She loved it and loved showing her children or friends around when we came down."

Ben learned a lot from his mother's experience. "I would say that in addition to my mother being very open to new experiences and different cultures, I think most of the successful expats 1) don't have great/tremendous attachments to where they are leaving. They (may not need) to be really close to their family or lots of friends, and 2) are flexible about food, housing, and other people's approach to life. If you grew up in foreign country X and return, those may not count much. But you won't be living cheaply if you want to totally recreate your US lifestyle in a place like Costa Rica (or Mexico). Houses are different. Cars are expensive. Local food is different and some switching will be required. There is no Trader Joe's. Mexico has some Costcos I hear but not Costa Rica. If you want a 2500 square ft house with central air, you are defeating yourself trying to save money. If you are ok with a simple two-bedroom, walking distance to the beach, with an air conditioner in one bedroom window you are much more likely to be happy. If you want a CT or MRI the first time you have a headache, you are going to be disappointed or broke soon."

Ben adds this observation as the adult child of an expat: "My mother's experience was positive for her, for her mother, and frankly for her children, because she basically organized it to take care of herself in her old age. Plus, her children, their spouses, and all the grandchildren, all went down to Costa Rica and were shown a good and interesting time for 10+ years of visits when she was still running around."

ADVICE FROM THE EXPERT EXPATS

One of the top picks for countries for retirees is Ecuador. Coincidently that is where our interviewees Edd and Cynthia Staton are living now.

We were fortunate enough to come across Edd and Cynthia Staton of Retirement Reimagined. Edd and Cynthia have been featured in numerous media outlets including US News and World Report, CNBC, and USA Today among many others. Edd and Cynthia have a program that helps people make the transition to living abroad. Their website is: www.eddandcynthia.com

Our interview with Edd and Cynthia was enlightening and we hope you enjoy it as much as we did:

Of all the countries you could have chosen, why Ecuador?
Before beginning research on potential countries, we created a Wish List of the most important factors that would be found in our new home abroad. The list included 1) low cost of living, 2) temperate climate, 3) proximity to the US, 4) excellent and affordable health care, 5) modern conveniences and cultural amenities, and 6) pedestrian lifestyle. Our home for the past decade, Cuenca, Ecuador, checked all the boxes.

What was the most unexpected or unanticipated (both good and bad) thing that happened after your move?
Our circumstances leaving the States were quite dire financially and we so hoped the situation would be better moving to Ecuador. We were therefore thrilled by how quickly we thrived in our new home. With the financial stress lifted we enthusiastically embraced every opportunity to enjoy life, make new friends, and get involved with local businesses and charities. On the flip side, nothing can prepare you for living in the mañana culture. Appointments being "suggestions" was extremely hard to wrap our North American brains around. We have since discovered that the whole idea of "right now" is highly overrated.

Have you participated in the health insurance program in Ecuador? How would you evaluate the medical system and care in Ecuador compared to the US?
Yes, we are members of Ecuador's national health care system. We have 100% coverage with $0 deductible and no restrictions for age

or pre-existing conditions. Our combined monthly premium is less than $90. We find the level of care here to be superior in many ways to what we've experienced in the US. In major cities, the facilities and equipment are top-notch. Physicians are often bilingual and have trained abroad. There is much less bureaucracy (doctors often have no staff!). And we really appreciate the conservative approach taken regarding the prescribing of drugs.

If one or both of you requires more care do you plan on staying in Ecuador?
Since we maintain our Medicare coverage we're blessed with having options depending on the situation. We'll cross that bridge when we come to it.

We've read that you did not speak the language when you moved to Ecuador. Do you now?
"Becoming fluent in a foreign language" was *not* on our Wish List. We are satisfied that we are now functional in Spanish. Also, there are many more English-speaking locals that we expected.

What's the #1 mistake that you see others who want to be expats do?
Deciding to relocate abroad based on where you like to vacation. You go on vacation somewhere to *get away* from your daily life, not for it to *become* your daily life. You can ignore many negatives about a place when you're only there for a short period. Not so when it's your 24/7/365 home.

What is the best way for someone to choose a country and then a specific region or town in a non-US country to live in during their retirement?
Besides, enroll in ***Retirement Reimagined***? ☺ 1) Do an internal profile to decide what you want your life to look like 2) Make a Wish List as per #1 above 3) Use that list to narrow down the possibilities regarding countries and locations within those countries 4) Take a scouting trip (or multiple trips if you are undecided and have the time/money) to make sure the place speaks to your heart, and that there are no deal-breakers lurking that your online research didn't reveal.

You live in Cuenca, Ecuador, voted several years in a row as the number one overseas retirement destination for North Americans by International Living magazine. Do you live in a neighborhood with other expats? Do you recommend being close and interacting more with the expat community?

Our neighborhood has very few expats. We've never found the area of town where most expats live to be very appealing. Since we shipped our belongings, our decision about where to live was based mainly on finding a place that would comfortably hold a 40' container full of our stuff. Unless you desire to be a pioneer or live "off the grid," we do recommend choosing a location with an established expat community. It makes the transition so much easier to have a built-in support network.

This is a delicate question and we will not put in the book if you prefer: Do you have any concerns about the current immigration issues in the US impacting your safety in Ecuador or for expats in other Central American or South American countries?

In Ecuador, immigration issues have recently been focused on how to successfully deal with the massive influx of refugees from Venezuela. Immigrants from the US continue to be welcomed. The countries in Central America most affected by US policies like Honduras and Guatemala are very poor and have few American expats. We always say that living abroad isn't a prison sentence. If you feel unsafe wherever you are, the choice to leave is always there.

How often do you return to the US?

Usually three times a year – spring, fall, and the holiday season.

WHAT HAPPENED TO EDD AND CYNTHIA WHEN COVID HIT?

As of May 31st, Edd and Cynthia were doing just fine. They were emerging from the same level of lockdown (with greater restrictions than many places in the US) that all of us have experienced, and there has been a flattening of the curve. Things were starting to slowly open up in Ecuador, but with safety protocols in place.

Edd and Cynthia report that the virus did not affect their income and since they work from home anyway, things have stayed remarkably stable for them. They have had to postpone a family trip to the states, and it is unknown when they can re-schedule that.

WHAT TO CONSIDER BEFORE MAKING THE LEAP

There are plenty of websites and articles that will spell out things to consider before making the leap into another country. We will summarize those here to give you pause before deciding. It's easy to overlook possible challenges when you dream of the good life abroad!

- **Take a sober look at the political situation.** The political climate in international countries is ever-changing. Your view of a country that once had a stable reputation may now be completely different. A good place to start is the US State Department.[28] Also, Investopedia is considered a neutral and reliable source of information. They have an article on the best countries for retirement abroad.[29]
- **Consider the requirements for living abroad.** No, you can't just pack your stuff and hop on a plane to set up shop in another country! There is lots of paperwork and other criteria such as minimum yearly income requirements. A good place to start is the US State Department which has all US embassies and consulates.[30]
- **Want to buy your dream home abroad?** Think again. Some countries, like New Zealand, make it very difficult to purchase a home. Forbes has a great article on some of the complexities of homeownership as well as the best countries to move to in 2019.[31] Most people rent. Many countries also allow for a 3-month visitor visa so you can test drive a place before making a permanent commitment.
- **What about healthcare?** Some countries will allow a new resident from the US to opt into the country's healthcare plan. Medicare does not cover medical care abroad. The cost of medical care abroad can be significantly lower than that of the U.S.

- **You still have to pay US taxes.** At least on your retirement income.
- **Language may be a barrier.** Unless you are fluent in the language of the country you are moving to, not knowing the language could be a barrier. Many people say it is not a deal-breaker, but having a serviceable command of the language will endear you to the locals. It will also help you get what you need when you need it!
- **Missing friends and family.** Yes, there is Skype and any number of other ways to stay in touch. But, don't underestimate the impact of not being able to see people personally, unless you make periodic visits back to the states.

PROS AND CONS OF BECOMING AN EXPAT:

PROS-

- Your retirement funds could last longer in some countries, but not all. Check this out thoroughly before deciding.
- You can experience a new start at an old age.

CONS-

- Moving to another country takes much more preparation and planning than a move to another state.
- You and your family will likely spend less time together if you are living in another country.
- You will have to learn the various official rules for non-citizens of the country you want to live in. You will have to deal with another level of red tape that does not exist for you in the US.

THIS IS FOR YOU IF:

- You have a sense of adventure and aren't afraid of learning a new culture.
- You have some experience traveling in other countries.

- You have a flexible nature-one that can roll with unanticipated challenges.

- The idea of making your retirement funds last longer by living in a less expensive country is appealing.
- You don't mind being away from friends and family and have
a plan in mind in how to stay connected.

STAY CLEAR IF:

- You are nervous and prefer predictability in your life.
- You have concerns about the quality of healthcare in another
country.
- You need to be near your friends and family for social
connection.
- Other cultures are intimidating to you. Especially the idea of
learning another language.
- The idea of not being able to travel freely back into the United
States is a frightening prospect.

7

WHAT IF IT DOESN'T WORK OUT? WHY EACH OF US NEEDS A PLAN B

"Life belongs to the living," wrote Johann Wolfgang von Goethe, "and he who lives must be prepared for changes."

You may have heard the saying that getting old is better than the alternative. Well, that may be true but most of us can agree that we want to get old on our own terms. We want to age with our wits about us and our bodies intact. That may indeed happen to many of us. Amanda recently heard a friend tell of her 92-year-old father who is in a hiking group and hiked four miles the other day. Athletic feats of aging seem to be hitting the media daily.

We know now that some of the aging process is in our control. The research is overwhelming at this point: exercise, eat a plant-based diet, work on balance, and stay social. Yet, despite our best efforts, the infirmities of aging can happen to anyone – a fall, a late diagnosis of a chronic medical condition, cancer, or any number of other unexpected medical events.

Human nature is a strong determinant of decision making. And, it is human nature to defer decisions about aging until something goes wrong. Unfortunately, that approach can have stressful, and expensive consequences. We have seen countless times that older people and their families will wait until a crisis to make life-changing decisions. Most of those times, they each had more than an inkling that help was already needed. The decision-making process becomes much more stressful when made in a hurry.

TIME FOR A REALITY CHECK

In this chapter, we challenge you to a reality check. In spite of our best efforts to maintain good health, some of us as we age are going to need help with personal care. That means that you will need someone to help you do activities that you normally don't even think about.

Health care professionals often refer to "activities of daily living." These are things that we take for granted. Every day you get up, you go to the bathroom, you get dressed, you walk, you make food for yourself and you eat. You turn off the stove and the lights. You sit down in a chair, you get up from a chair, you walk up and down steps. You talk with other people, you make phone calls to tell others what you need. You manage your finances and you clean your home. You take your medications when you are supposed to and go to see your doctor when scheduled. You get in a car or a subway, you shop, you get your haircut. You brush your teeth, you get in comfortable night-clothes, get in bed, and go to sleep.

Now imagine that you cannot do one or a combination of the activities of daily living listed above. You can walk to the kitchen, but you can't lift the heavy pan to cook in or reach the shelves to get food out of the cupboard. You can walk to the mailbox but are too tired or confused to open the mail when you get back inside. You can't hear the phone when it is ringing. Driving gets scary and downright dangerous. You either cannot negotiate the shower or are scared to get in it. It takes an hour or more to get dressed, and you decide to sleep in your clothes. And, worst of all, you can slowly walk to the bathroom, but you cannot wipe yourself.

Any of these changes can result in needing another person to help you. Yes, we have some tech solutions to help; there are robotic helpers for some limited tasks. These continue to need improvement to be considered truly effective. Overall, though, the best help continues to be another person.

We could spend a lot of time talking about the indignities of growing old. In our field, we are very empathetic and understanding of the psychological impact of changes that people experience. However, for the purposes of this book and the task at hand, we are focusing on planning.

For most of this book, we are discussing your most active and independent phase of aging. We wish for all of us that this phase is very long and unending. However, we advise you to think ahead and be prepared if it is short-lived. What do you want your care to look like?

One thing that we have learned in working with older adults and mental health is that those who plan ahead for themselves are more satisfied with the outcome. From our experience, people who end up in a situation in which others decide for them where they will live and who will care for them tend to be much less happy. Numerous studies have shown that the transition into care is associated with developing depression.[32] This is sometimes referred to as "Transition or Transfer Trauma"[33] and can result in a number of unpleasant personality and physical changes.

The best way to avoid or at least decrease the negative impact is for you to be involved in the planning. If you can no longer take care of yourself, where will you move to? Or, if you can stay in your current home, how will your care be managed?

The other big question that must go hand in hand with your planning is: How will you pay for it? To answer that question, educate yourself about the costs of care. Know what your insurance will cover and what costs will be your responsibility. If you can, prepare a "worst-case scenario" budget that considers a wide range of care options. For ideas and resources, a good website to start with is https://www.payingforseniorcare.com/. Another great site is Genworth. They provide state by state cost of care for everything from home care to nursing home. https://www.genworth.com/aging-and-you/finances/cost-of-care.html.

AMANDA'S "START AT THE END AND GO BACKWARDS" APPROACH TO PLANNING

Amanda likes to say that you should start at the end and go backward with your planning. Where is the end? Not to be morbid, but the end is the worst-case scenario. For many people this means ending up in a nursing home needing the maximum amount of help. If you plan for that, then you will have most everything covered. It is human nature to put off thinking about what could go wrong, but trying to plan when it does go wrong can leave you woefully unprepared.

What does it look like to start at the end? We suggest the following guidelines and questions to discuss, as a family. The more your family knows about what you want (and it is in writing) the best chance you have of your wishes being followed.

1. The worst-case scenario for most people is nursing home care. Although it may be unlikely, plan for it. It is very expensive. Some people take out long term care policies. Others have the financial resources to pay out of pocket or deplete their resources until they qualify for Medicaid.

2. Regardless of age, prepare advance directives that designate a trusted healthcare proxy. This person can advocate for you and carry out your wishes should you become incapacitated. No one knows when the end of their life will be. Advance directives also allow you to state what medical interventions you want should you need life-saving treatment.

3. If you need help when you age, who will provide that help? Do you expect family members to help and if so have you discussed this with them? If you are willing to get professional help in your home, educate yourself about what insurance pays for and what it doesn't. Most people who need care end up paying for that care due to the limits of insurance coverage. If you are adamant about staying home as you age, calculate that cost based on current rates.

4. For many people, the cost of in-home care starts to creep up as they need more hours of help and eventually exceeds the price of assisted living. For example, you may need 4-8 hours of help a day and can afford it. When you need 24 hour/ seven days a week home care, the cost exceeds what you would pay for assisted living. Evaluate your finances in light of this possibility. And don't forget to assess the fact that you could live into your 90's.

5. Take a clear, realistic look at your aging. Assess your current health and commit to improving areas that you can. This may include increasing your activity level, paying attention to

diet, hydration, and stress management. Focus on what you can control.

6. Last, and not least, after you have done everything you can to plan for the worst, live your life to the best. That means assessing what is important. Take responsibility for your health, and envision the kind of community you want as you age.

THE BEAUTY OF ADVANCE DIRECTIVES

It can be hard for people in their 50's or 60's to picture themselves not being able to speak up and say what they want. It may be hard to imagine that you cannot completely control your privacy, your residence, and what you will eat and drink. But, a variety of medical events that are common in aging can create exactly the conditions that would prevent you from basic communication.

Fortunately, you can put it in writing. Using the legal document called an advance directive mentioned in the last section, you can specify what you want and what you don't want. Not only does the advance directive spell out one's wishes for medical care at the end of life, it can lso contain information about what your preferences are for living with care. Please consult your attorney and make sure that you get the appropriate forms completed as directed by law in your state.

Suppose you always hated that place that your great-Aunt Maxine lived in at the end of her life. You can specify that you should absolutely not be placed there in the event that you need full-time care. Maybe you and a friend have always agreed that if you have to live with help, you would pool resources and live together with a caregiver. You can put the plan, the names, and contact information in your advance directive. You can describe Plan B for if you need assistance. And, you can state what would be least objectionable to you if you needed full-time care.

Now, we need to clarify. Having this plan in a legal document such as an advance directive does not guarantee that it will be carried out. There may not be funds for your plan at the time you need it. Your friend that you planned to live with and share care may have predeceased you. Having a basic plan, however, will give whoever is trying to help you an idea of what you prefer and hopefully get as close to that as possible.

The next point that we want to emphasize is to communicate with your family what is in your advance directive. This document is a great starting point for a conversation about the future with your spouse or partner, your children, and any significant family member or friends. So many families avoid these important planning sessions. You can buck the trend. You can get a head start by sitting down with the people who are closest to you and telling them what you want and where to find your legal documents.

Finally, it is always possible that you might change your mind about some aspect of your advance directive. Here are some tips:

- Remember to review your plan about every 3-5 years and more often as you get older.
- There may be a new facility or care opportunity that did not exist when you made your original plan. Or the place that you had in mind has gone out of business. Adjust as needed.
- Communicate with your family if you make any changes and to remind them that you are stating what you would prefer.

INTERVIEW WITH LUANN

Luann is a 55-year-old married woman who lives with her husband and works in a university setting. She has three grown children and two grandchildren. We wanted to know about her plans for aging, what she feels prepared for and what worries her the most.

Do you have any health problems and if so what are those?
We have no major health problems. I have slightly elevated blood pressure which is controlled by medication, diet, and exercise.

What is your vision for aging? Aging in place or with other people? Have you or your friend's considered alternative options? Co-housing/golden girls/ renting as a group/ co-ownership. What about assisted living?
My vision is to stay in my home for as long as possible. If I get to the point that I can no longer safely be in my home, I would see assisted living as the next step.

Have you considered the financial implications of aging? What is your health insurance and how will you pay for care if you need it in the future?
I have considered the financial implications of aging and quite frankly it worries me! All of the unknowns. My current health insurance is offered through my employer. Again...unknown what insurance will look like when I retire. At this point, I envision that I will have some form of Medicare and buy a supplemental policy to help cover the costs not covered by my Medicare policy.

Do you think you have a clear picture of what Medicare pays for and what it doesn't?
Yes, I think I have a pretty clear picture of what Medicare pays for, and know that I have options for Medicare Part D for prescription drug coverage. I know it does NOT cover long term care and assisted living expenses. And also does not cover dental expenses.

What is your biggest concern about aging?
Not having the financial resources to be comfortable. I find it very hard to know how much money to plan. We do have a financial planner and feel like we are somewhat on track, but I also feel that they don't know what the future brings either. And we do have our investments diversified but during these volatile times, I still see our accounts losing a significant amount of money. I know long term things balance out. But the closer I get to retirement the more I worry we will have enough.

Do you expect that your children will help take care of you?
I do think my children would be willing on some level to help us. Mostly I would envision that if we needed help with being driven to doctor appointments or have them grocery shopping for us, things like that. I would never envision living with them and would not expect that.

Have you discussed your plans for your children taking care of you as you age?
Oh goodness, that is a good question! I have not discussed plans in detail at all! They certainly know of our advance directives and the

medical aspect if something happens to us. But we have not talked
about natural aging and if we can no longer care for ourselves in our
home. And if I am being completely honest, not something I had
even thought about discussing until I get quite a bit older, like maybe
at retirement age.

*Have you and your husband ever considered a long term care policy to help
pay for future care needs?*
I did consider a long term policy years ago but never followed
through. And I think they are hard to come by now. This definitely
isn't the best answer but...I have always envisioned that our retirement savings plus the sale of our house would help fund a long term
care/assisted living situation. I do know how incredibly expensive assisted living is and how quickly it can go. My personal belief is that
what I have worked for can help support me. I don't feel that I need
to have money to leave my children when I die. So if I spend it all, so
be it. Anything that is left they are welcome to it.

*Do you know of anyone who is living in co-housing, renting or co-owning/
Multigenerational?*
I do not at this point. I have a group of friends that we joke we will
move to "Silly Villa" as a group. But purely tongue and cheek.

Do you have advance directives in place?
Yes, I do have advance directives in place.

Any other thoughts about aging?
I just want to let you know I also have some personal beliefs over
choice when it comes to end of life care. My wish for the future is
that we all have the choice of Physician Aid in Dying (Death with
Dignity or whatever it will be called) if the time presents itself that
way. I watched both of my parents and others die a very long drawn
out death, spending a great deal of money on futile treatments at the
end of their life. I know my parents would not have chosen to use this
and end their own life on their terms. And none of us really know
what we will do when faced with that decision. BUT...I would like
the choice. And I feel that knowing what I have experienced, if I had

a terminal condition that was going to greatly affect my quality of life, I might make a choice to end it peacefully and on my terms.

ROXANNE'S STORY

Roxanne, age 63, and her husband Ted, age 69, are a pair of lovebirds who enjoy each other's company completely. They are also fortunate in that they both are passionate about their professional careers. Roxanne has worked in many areas of the arts and has her own arts consulting business that has taken years to grow. This requires a great deal of travel and she is always on the go. Ted is a health care professional who has a warm regard and respect for all of his patients. His commitment to them is genuine and inspiring. They both love their work and continue to take on new projects. They also love the outdoors and have traveled together for work and pleasure. They do not have children of their own, but have had substantial roles in helping raise nieces and nephews.

They realize that they have worked really hard, but want to make sure that they will still have time to travel together. They both plan on slowing down to part-time work in the next five years. They have also considered downsizing to a smaller home, but have not found anything that appeals to them yet. Roxanne says, "our home is much too large for us, but we love it. Our open basement has, what could be, an ideal two-bedroom apartment. We might convert the house into a disguised duplex, but this wouldn't happen for another 8-10 years. Then the upstairs would be perfect for us until we are forced to move for health reasons."

As far as considering the worst case scenario, Roxanne and Ted have consulted a financial advisor. They are going to start a long term care policy and have learned about Medicare and supplemental insurance. They have also had frank conversations about aging and health. Roxanne recounts that they have discussed lots of details. The beginning of the COVID pandemic was a motivating factor. "We've considered death, DNR orders, and cremation so I think we're on the same page with that. We've assigned a trusted family member to be in charge of our estate. We were prompted by the virus to think about this and to start the process to get these things in some semblance of order. After handling my father's estate, which was in impeccable order, it was still hard and so much more work than I had anticipated. We are trying to make this easy for our heirs and to be sure that things go where we want them to go." They are both philosophical about if there is a downturn in their finances. "We might not get to do some of the incredible hikes we had hoped to do, but we can garden, read books and do things that are important to us that don't cost money."

Not having children has added another layer of concern about aging. Roxanne puts it this way: "I think for both of us, it is that we didn't have children, so who do we turn to for help? Of course, this is too big of a burden for children too. We have trusted nieces and nephews that might not be able to help us that much, but they can perhaps oversee our care. This is something to ponder."

While Roxanne admires the creativity of housing ideas such as cohousing, she does not see that as an option for herself. "I never had a roommate in college and I realize, again with the virus, that I'm an unabashed introvert and cherish my alone time." She did admire some relatives who lived as homesharers. "I had three elderly great aunts who outlived their husbands and bought a beautiful home together. They had wonderful dinner parties, tea in the afternoon with white gloves and it was always a pleasure to go to their home. They had beautiful gardens and one became a nice artist. They didn't have a lot of money, but they were healthy and managed a wonderful life."

A WORD ABOUT COVID-19 AND PLAN B

The impact on COVID-19 on people over 65 has been enormous and in many cases, fatal. Older adults and their families have been horrified by how this deadly infection has spread through nursing homes and some assisted living communities. At the same time, as the shutdown took place, few could anticipate how the elderly have been literally held prisoner in their own homes and prevented from spending any time in person with family and friends.

As we write this, answers to many pandemic questions are still unanswered. How long will elder adults be forced to live in isolation? Will there be effective treatments and vaccines? Will increased contact with family and friends be safe? And, will the epidemic of loneliness among the old that already existed prior to the pandemic proliferate?

We do not pretend to have the answers. But, during this time, we have noticed that some people managed to make the best of their living situation as the shutdown approached. Others moved to a location that was better for them. It was like a creepy version of musical chairs. Quick, where will you stay before the door closes you in or out?

You might think of this as having a "disaster plan." Some things are simply not affordable or practical for all people. But, we think that ideas are useful as a starting point to discuss with your support system in the event of a similar disaster:

- Some people who were living in care settings moved back in with family before the doors slammed shut. We do not imply that this works for every family. It does not. Most people living in care settings such as nursing homes or assisted living are not doing it as their first choice. But, if there are enough people in a family unit who can pitch in to provide care, this is an option. The benefit is that the older person is not in isolation and family members are not prevented from visiting them when they need them most.
- People in some urban environments left the city to live in a second home. Consider if you, a friend or someone in your extended family has access to spare space. This could be an additional home, an accessory dwelling unit in their yard, a spare room over the garage in the suburbs. Even if temporary, it could be a safe haven physically and psychologically.
- If you live alone and independently and have room for another person, invite them to shelter in place (SIP) with you. It could be a long haul by yourself. Yes, we hear of people who have done this and are getting annoyed with daily life with a dear friend. But, as one 60-something who is SIP alone said to us recently "I haven't touched another human being in months. Not a hug, or a hand on a shoulder. It makes me feel so sad."
- If you are choosing to live now or in the future in assisted

living or a nursing home, vet them for COVID and infectious disease plans. Consider a smaller facility or at least one that has smaller groupings of residents to live in a "pod" or family-style space. Have they made changes to the design or how care is provided since the pandemic? Ask about how they treat their staff, what their pay scale is, and what the turnover rate is.

A PRE-COVID OPTION WORTH A CLOSER LOOK

Prior to COVID, a family told us that they had found the perfect boarding home for their elder family member. On closer inspection, it turned out to be a very unique assisted living facility. We hope that more assisted living facilities take the cue from this example to make group living more like home. With the perspective of the pandemic, this design answers the need for smaller groupings, more consistent staffing and care. Read more about this creative option.

JOYCE'S STORY

Joyce continued to live in her family home after her husband passed away. However, as her memory became less reliable, she and her family agreed that she would move in with one of her sons nearby. This worked really well for the family, including Joyce's daughter, Jane. Jane lived close to her brother's neighborhood. She could drop in to visit with her mother for 5 minutes or for the afternoon when she was off work. She could easily pick her mother up for doctor's appointments or for other outings.

As her mother's memory problems and confusion grew, however, Jane and her brothers became more concerned about the hours that she was alone. They began to search for a place where she would have more supervision than they could provide with their work schedules.

They found what they initially thought of as a boarding home. In a quiet residential neighborhood in the suburbs of a large metropolitan area, the residence is in a large multi-bedroom, 3 car garage home. It provides meals and an onsite caregiver with one assistant. The total number of seniors in residence varies from 6-8 people.

The home had been modified to care for people with mobility issues. There is a stairlift on each of the house's stairs, making all levels accessible. There are several residents who are in wheelchairs. The family dining room is the site of all the meals throughout the day. The living room is large and is where residents gather to watch TV and have some activities such as art projects or music. The backyard has a deck for the residents and looks out onto a golf course, a beautiful green space.

The home is part of the Robin's Nest in the Chicago suburbs. While the Robin's Nest includes a traditional, larger, assisted living facility, it also maintains a network of several smaller scale, assisted living homes that are housed in actual former single-family structures in neighborhoods nearby. Started by a doctor, these homes have a much smaller number of residents and a truly home-like feel.

Jane describes her mother's transition to living in this home as very smooth. Joyce and her children have a good rapport with the primary caregiver in the home. Joyce is still ambulatory and remembers her children when they come to visit. She enjoys hearing about their workday but does not remember the conversations an hour later. Joyce's private bedroom is on the basement level and is small. She shares a bathroom with another person who lives in the second bedroom on that floor. This did not pose a concern and she adjusted to this well. She spends the majority of her day on the main level in the dining and living room area.

Joyce has been at the Robin's Nest home for a year and half. She is in her 90's and is now on hospice care. Jane says that other residents have passed away at the home. Her family anticipates that she will be able to stay there until the end.

WILL SENIOR HOUSING WITH CARE CHANGE AFTER COVID?

The damage of the coronavirus pandemic to the medical model of nursing homes around the world is still being assessed. But, many are eager to find a redesign that will provide greater safety from infections and greater quality of life.

There is no getting around the fact that older people still need the option of housing with care. Whether an assisted living that offers "care-lite" or a complete skilled nursing facility, some people cannot live without them. There is an entire industry, mostly profit-driven, that provides this care. The pandemic has provided the opportunity for the public to become aware of the pitfalls of that care. We have seen the headlines and the tragedies. We understand that how these places are run has a huge impact on the health and welfare of the residents and the staff alike.

We will not try to predict what changes, if any, will occur in the care homes of the future. We do know that there is tremendous discussion and ideas are in the pipeline. We encourage you to ask direct questions of any place that you are considering to live. Find out what they have changed or re-designed to reduce the spread of infections and improve care and quality of life. Each person has to decide what is most important to them in making these decisions. Is it freedom at the expense of community or community at the expense of freedom?

DESIGNING PLAN B – PROS AND CONS

PROS:

- People who make a plan for their future and aging tend to feel more control over their life.
- Having a detailed plan gives you a sober view of what may await you as you age. This will prepare you to be more psychologically flexible. If you are prepared for change, you may adjust more easily.
- Planning for retirement and aging sooner allows you to save whatever amount of money that you can. Even small amounts over time can grow into the cushion that you will need.

CONS:

- You feel ill-equipped and intimidated by the idea of planning. Seek help: Many senior centers provide planning education, identify resources and forms.
- You want to plan, but don't have children or someone that you

trust to put into the position of power of attorney or trustee. Again, check with your senior center or local aging services to get advice and direct you to legal resources.

- Thinking about and planning for aging is overwhelming. You have too many other responsibilities to worry about something far into the future.

THIS IS FOR YOU IF:

- You want to have greater control over where you live and who will care for you if you should need it.
- You believe getting the information in advance helps you make better decisions.
- You love your family, but you want to make sure that they know and understand what your wishes are while you are still able to tell them yourself.

STAY CLEAR IF:

- The thought of making a plan for the worst-case scenario sends you into a panic attack.
- You feel more confident that your children, spouse, or relative will do a better job taking care of these details than you would.

8

SUPER AGERS ROLL WITH THE PUNCHES

In Chapter Seven, we talk about the how's and why's of being prepared for aging. Life can come at you fast at any age, but the older you get, the harder it can be to get back on your feet. The personality characteristics of flexibility and resilience are the necessary ingredients to cope with unexpected changes. To roll with the punches, you have to be adaptable.

"You've got to tell them to be prepared. They're going to get old." This was the sage advice from a family member of Leslie's when she heard the concept of this book. Aunt Mimi and her husband, Howard, should know. They are the living embodiment of successful contingency planning. Now in their mid-90's and still, comparatively, going strong, they have lived to tell the tale.

WHEN YOUR FINANCIAL SAFETY NET DISAPPEARS

Shortly after retiring at age 65 with a full pension in the late 1980s, Howard's company went bankrupt. Overnight, their pension disappeared. With many years of hard work and watching that pension grow, they had dreamed about when they would finally have time to enjoy life and do what they really wanted to do. Avid travelers, they planned to spend that pension and their "golden years" exploring the world. Those dreams vanished in a flash. They had some savings but mostly were left to survive on social security.

But, this amazing couple who met and fell in love when they were both serving in the Navy in WWII, did not fold up and crumple. They sat down and got organized. As children of the depression, they were no strangers to frugal living.

First, they realized that they had to sell their house. This house was where they had lived for many years and raised their child. It had been their family neighborhood. They had forged relationships with neighbors, schools, and friends. It was a tough decision. They had worked hard over many years to raise the money to build the house. Both Mimi and Howard are artistic people. They had worked with the architect and loved the design. Their two story, three bedroom house, and the yard was a space that they had personally helped to create. However, their financial safety net had dissolved and they knew it was a sacrifice that they had to make.

As they searched in less expensive neighborhoods nearby for a more affordable place to live, something lucky happened. There was a condominium building that looked somehow familiar and appealing to them. It happened to have been designed and built by the same architect who planned their house. They found a unit that was a smaller version of their home. It had many of the same visual elements of their beloved house. It was in a building with an elevator and while most of the living space was on one floor, there was even a downstairs guest room and bath for their son to stay when he visited.

The couple was able to settle and embrace their new, pared-down life. Their zest for living and exploring the world, however, had not abandoned them. The question was, how could they afford to see the world?

After a time, they heard from friends who were spending the winter in San Miguel de Allende, Mexico. San Miguel de Allende is in the central highlands of the country and is a thriving center of arts and culture. It is the home of an international artist community and attracts many foreign visitors and expats. Their friends wanted Mimi and Howard to join them as "snowbirds" (people from a northern climate who spend the winters in a warm southern climate.) Not only did this appeal to them as world travelers, it offered a respite from the harsh winter of their northeastern state. The couple looked into the costs. The only way they could swing it would be if they could rent out their condo while they were away.

Remember that this was in the 1980's. There was no Airbnb. Mimi and Howard mentioned their thoughts to friends. Through word of mouth, another friend contacted them. She had a relative, a man who was relocating to their urban area from another part of the country for his company. He was very interested in renting their condo. It would give him a place to transition and time to find a permanent home with less pressure.

In a matter of weeks, their hoped-for trip became a reality. At that time, homeowner's associations had less restrictive requirements. They did not have to have approval for renting their apartment. They set a price for the rent and required that the full amount, two months rent plus a security deposit, be paid in advance. Howard installed extra shelves into a closet and put on a security lock. Mimi and Howard put their most cherished and fragile possessions and sensitive documents into this locked closet. They emptied a clothes closet in the master bedroom for the tenant. They packed simply and headed to Mexico.

When in Mexico, Howard and Mimi made friends with locals and expats alike. They took art classes, including jewelry making, painting and sculpture. They had dinner parties and shopped in the local food markets. They loved it there. And the rent that they charged for their condo covered all of their expenses.

Back from their trip, they lived frugally. They made sure to share with their network of friends that their condo would be available again the following winter. Again, there was a short term tenant who loved the location and was able to pay upfront. They extended to 3 months away.

Mimi and Howard were able to afford to travel to Mexico to avoid the cold for 19 winters. Sometimes the tenant would be a middle-aged person who was going through a divorce. They needed a good apartment near their work while they adjusted to the change in their life. Other times, the renter would be a person moving from another state and unfamiliar with their city. They appreciated staying in a real home while they learned their way around. Almost always, the person was someone referred by a friend or was a niece or nephew of someone they knew and trusted. And, there was never any variation about getting the entire payment upfront.

Towards the end of this treasured yearly travel, the couple decided to change from Mexico to Florida. Their son and his wife had moved to Florida and they wanted to spend time with them. Some of their friends in San Miguel de Allende had stopped going or had passed away. They made a new friend in the landlord of the small apartment they rented in Florida. They stayed at this same apartment for several years.

Eventually, Mimi and Howard found that though they were in pretty good health, they were slowing down a little. In their early 90's, they decided that these big trips were over. Friends were dying and they didn't know as many of their neighbors. They decided that it was time to move to a more structured home while they could still take advantage of activities and amenities. They had friends who lived at a certain senior retirement home. This one is huge, with beautiful walking trails, an indoor pool, and an active recreation calendar. It's almost like a little village of its own. They went to take a look and decided to move. They chose a 2 bedroom apartment.

Once again, they sold their much-loved condo and downsized. Mimi, an avid cook, got rid of all of her timeworn cookbooks and all but her favorite cookware. "What do I need them for? We have to pay to eat in the dining room at least once a day. I'll still do some cooking, of course. If I want a recipe, I'll look it up on the internet." For both of them, the most important feature of their apartment is the artwork that has been the heart of each of their homes. They have created most of this art themselves. It is what makes their home a home.

Soon after moving in and making friends, Mimi and Howard were appointed ambassadors of the community. Their volunteer job is to welcome new residents to the building, invite them to join them for dinners in the dining hall, introduce them to clubs and new friends. And, in so doing, they have made even more friends. They each have group activities that they enjoy doing with their neighbors. Howard still drives occasionally to Trader Joe's, and they both go to a cousin's holiday dinner nearby. Their son and his wife come to visit them there from Florida.

Mimi and Howard are still in the apartment. Now they are 96 and 97. While each has had some health scares, overall, they are both remarkably healthy and mobile. They have the peace of mind, however, that should they need assistive care, it is an option in their three levels of care facility. They will not have to move anywhere else.

WHAT HAPPENED TO MIMI AND HOWARD WHEN COVID HIT?

Mimi and Howard have adjusted very well to the restrictions of the pandemic. The retirement community has asked all residents to shelter in place in their apartments. The residents cannot go to the gorgeous dining rooms, so they are given a menu and order the day before. Meals are delivered once a day to the door. Mimi says it's way too much food, and she happily adds spices to make it more to their liking. Their annual health exams have been postponed a few months, but both are feeling well and are not concerned. The staff bring treats and do some serenading at the doorways to break the monotony. The couple is lucky that they can still go outside and enjoy the green space and walking trails. Their son calls every day. They have even learned to Zoom with extended family and loved seeing the nieces and nephews. Now, they might try some of the streaming activities and classes offered by the community. And, over time, the community has formed activity pods for bridge and other games. Mimi said it was a relief to be in the room with people she knows.

As you can see by this example and the others we have mentioned, older adults are generally resilient in times of stress or uncertainty. A lifetime of coping with unexpected changes brings a certain mindset that finds the positive in challenging circumstances.

Whether it is a pandemic, a change in health status, or family conflict, learning how to be more resilient is possible. But, it takes effort. It means accepting what you can't change and focusing on what you can.

FLEXIBILITY – NOT JUST FOR YOGA!

According to an entry on Wikipedia, flexibility is "a personality trait that describes the extent to which a person can cope with changes in circumstances and think about problems and tasks in novel, creative ways. This trait is used when stressors or unexpected events occur, requiring a person to change their stance, outlook, or commitment."[34]

Old people are not commonly thought of as flexible, physically, or mentally. There are many stereotypes of old people being stubborn, resistant, and "stuck in their ways." After a lifetime of experience, it makes sense that an individual knows what they like and don't like. They know what they want and see no reason to change that thinking.

As life expectancy expands, however, the advantages of having a flexible attitude as you age become clear. You may develop a chronic health condition that requires you to adjust your lifestyle. You may no longer be able to afford where you live. You may need to live closer to your family or friends. In other words, change happens to everyone, young and old.

In our work, we have seen issues arise for seniors and their families when there is a lack of flexibility. In our culture, we value the individual and rights and freedom. As one gets older, however, it gets harder to do whatever you want. Compromises can feel like humiliation to some. For the family, a stubborn older relative can appear to be just "digging in their heels." For that person, it may feel like everyone around them is trying to take their personal control away from them. And, changing circumstances can alter how much autonomy a person has.

But, there is nothing more isolating than saying "no" to every suggestion that is offered. Not only does saying "no" eliminate possibilities, but it also creates a barrier. People of all ages can do this. Think of someone you know who has a tendency to say "Yes, but…" when others offer suggestions to solve a problem. That person has already lined up reasons why something will not work for them. They are never really considering the option at hand and have already decided "no" in advance. They may also be fending off the help of others in order to maintain complete control.

Resistance of this type is also very energy-consuming. It's like being on offense and defense at the same time. You are always fighting a battle. And, while you are fighting, you may be losing valuable ground.

Saying "yes" to every idea, of course, is not always the solution. However, an intention to keep an open mind can open doors. A great way to start is to say "maybe."

Consider the following story. It is of a real person who was faced with numerous life changes and decisions to make as he aged. He could have said no. But, he said yes.

A TRAVELER OF THE WORLD
CREATES AN AGING JOURNEY

In many ways, Dick had always been prepared to keep moving. Throughout his life, he was curious and seeking new experiences. He always looked for ways to meet new people and explore different cultures. Though he started his life in the Midwest of the United States, Dick traveled to many places in his lifetime. As a young man, he moved to Japan following World War II to teach English to young Japanese people. He made many friends and discovered the commonalities between people who had so recently been at war. He studied history and enjoyed a career as an educator around the country in both high schools and higher-level education. He became an author and valued family and community member.

Aging was no different for Dick. After raising a family in Washington DC in a four-story Victorian home, Dick and his wife continued to live there and pursued their interests and travels. Dick's wife passed away in 2004. He had to make a decision about where he would live. Consulting with his adult daughters who both lived in other states, they decided together to do a major downsize. Instead of moving away from the family home, however, Dick and his family emptied the top three floors of the house of all the family belongings. They converted the first floor of the house into Dick's new home. As part of this undertaking, they anticipated all of the needs of an aging person. Dick's daughter Susan, fortunately, is a certified aging-in-place specialist. She was able to bring her expertise in modifying and adapting an existing home to include universal design elements such as widened doorways and assistive equipment and design in the bathroom. After almost 2 years of completing this work, they rented the upper three floors of the Victorian home to a family. Dick's life continued at age 80 in the modified family home on the first floor and he took on a new role as a landlord.

This went well for about five years. Over time, the demands of being a landlord grew. Dick was not as happy with the arrangement as he initially had been. At the same time, Dick found out that he needed a hip replacement. The first doctor that he went to did not give him a great deal of confidence. When he discussed getting a second opinion with his daughter Susan, they came up with a completely different idea. They decided that maybe it was time for Dick to move on from the house in Washington DC. Susan lives in California. Dick and his wife had visited there many, many times and had fallen in love with the Santa Barbara area where Susan lived with her husband and two children. On their visits, they had made a number of friends, attended church services there, and loved the climate. Susan had connections with local doctors and asked her father if he wanted to come to live in Santa Barbara and get his hip replacement there. And that's exactly what he did.

Dick packed up all of his remaining belongings and moved across the country. He had a successful surgery and his mobility was much improved. As it happened, his grandson was looking for a place to live at the same time that Dick moved to Santa Barbara. They agreed to move in together. They found a home to rent together that was accessible for an older person to live comfortably and safely. Dick and his grandson truly enjoyed their time together living in that house. Dick was often found socializing with 20-somethings, with each gaining from the experience. Because Dick's family was now close by, they were more easily able to do things together than when they had only sporadic visits with each other. They went to musical events, they went out to dinner and they traveled together.

This arrangement lasted for about three and a half years. Then something happened that many renters dread. The landlord decided to sell the rental home. That meant that Dick and his grandson had to move out. At the time, Dick's grandson decided to find a place of his own. That meant that Dick had to find a new place to live on his own at age 89. Susan's husband was taking their dog for a walk about two blocks from their home and happened to see a For Lease sign in a new apartment building. They all went to look at the apartment and found that it was perfect for Dick. There was an elevator in the building, he had a great view, he had an accessible bathroom and the location could not be beat. Because of Susan's expertise in aging and knowledge of the possible risks as his age advanced, she got her father a Lifeline monitor that had GPS, a fall detector feature and that was waterproof so that her father could keep it on when he was in the shower. This gave her great peace of mind and she knew that she could get to her father quickly if she was notified.

During this part of Dick's life, he had many things that he enjoyed and explored. He continued to write about his experiences in Japan. He walked the couple of blocks to Susan's house every night for dinner. He was part of the community and he had friends. He and Susan even took a trip to Japan by boat. When they arrived they met with people who had been Dick's students decades before and also were in their 80s. It was a time of returning to roots and celebrating life.

When Dick was 92 years old, he and Susan were planning a train trip to Chicago to connect with old friends there. But things changed before that could happen. He called Susan one night and told her that he had terrible stomach pain. In the emergency room, the doctor sadly was able to quickly pinpoint the cause. Dick had pancreatic cancer. He was able to stay in his apartment and get hospice care. A close friend from Chicago came to him and stayed near him. He died with his family around him. Then, as had been previously planned, the family took that final three-day train trip to Chicago with Dick's ashes in a martini shaker. He made one last journey to have his ashes scattered where he started.

Clearly, Dick was a Super Ager. He was fortunate to have generally very good health and maintained clear thinking throughout his life. Even after having a hip replacement, he did not slow down. Not everyone will be this lucky. However, we have much to learn from his story. This was a person who knew where he wanted to live and how he wanted to live as he aged.

First, Dick was flexible about where he lived. He was open to the idea of completely rearranging his family home to accommodate another family to live there. He was willing to move across the country to be closer to his family. He was open to living with another generation, and then again to live alone.

He did not resist downsizing. Which is good, because he actually ended up doing that over and over again each time he moved.

Even though he was involved with downsizing each time he moved, Dick did not give up treasures that imparted special meaning for him. Remember that Dick had lived for a time as a young man in Japan? When he left Japan, he had a large number of Japanese river rocks shipped back home to the states. He later used these rocks to landscape a Japanese style garden in his backyard in Washington DC. When he later moved across the country to California, the rocks were on the moving van. They were used in his daughter Susan's garden since he moved into a rental. Susan thought that was their final move. However, after Dick passed away, she and her husband made a fun discovery. When her husband started moving a couple of Dick's potted plants from his last apartment, he thought that they were awfully heavy. When they uprooted the plants, they found that Dick had plenty of the Japanese rocks at the bottom of the planters. Sometimes a touchstone of home really is a stone!

As you can see from his story, Dick was a unique and strong individual. It is not every 80-something year old who is willing to pick up roots and move across the country. He also endured the precarious risks of being a tenant and had to move when his rental was sold. But with family support (and, of course, that may have been crucial to his success), he was able to move again. Each time, he moved to a smaller place. But, largely he maintained his independence and sense of self.

A PRO-ACTIVE APPROACH TO LIFE AND AGING WELL: PAT'S STORY

We have greatly enjoyed meeting people who seem to have the knack for looking ahead and making forward-thinking decisions. A great example is the following story of Pat. Notice how she doesn't avoid making the changes needed as her life advances. Health issues are taken in stride. At the same time, she has looked all the way through to the end, knows what she wants, and has clearly communicated with her family.

Earlier in her life, Pat lived as a divorced, working mother of two children in a single-family home with three bedrooms and a yard. The house was a historic home in a nice neighborhood. She was a longtime school teacher. "I was able to walk to my school from my home for over 20 years." As her daughters grew up, went to college and moved on into their own lives, Pat realized the house was too large for one person.

At age 59, Pat prepared her home to sell. At the same time, she began to look for a condominium to purchase and live in. She put a down payment on a new condo that was being built nearby in a thriving urban area. She was very excited about it. She liked the architecture and the downtown location. At the last minute, however, the developer notified her of a change in the design. Instead of a wrought-iron balcony enclosure, they were putting in a concrete pony wall. "That just didn't work for me," Pat says and she was able to get out of the deal.

She looked at another condominium development. Again, she came very close to signing the dotted line. And again, there were last-minute changes that did not suit her style.

By this point, her beloved house had been sold on October 31. The buyers were a new family who were eager to move in by Thanksgiving. Pat was not sure what she was going to do. With both of her condominium options dissolved she had no other ideas in place. Serendipity stepped in. Some parents of former students mentioned that they owned a fourplex apartment building near her neighborhood and had a vacancy. Pat went to look at the apartment and fell in love. "The apartment has south-facing windows which give me a lot of sunlight. There are beautiful hardwood floors. And even at my house I never had a garage. Here I do."

DOWNSIZING SOMETIMES HAPPENS IN STAGES

We asked Pat about the downsizing process. She laughed. "I got pneumonia." While Pat was looking at condominiums, she had dutifully started sorting, moving and throwing away household goods. But, when the house sold so quickly, she suddenly had to go into high gear. The one area of the house that she hadn't gotten to yet was the attic. There had been a fire some years before in her neighborhood and unbeknownst to Pat, ash and soot had unexpectedly gathered through the vents in her attic. Many of the boxes in the attic had been there since Pat and her ex-husband moved to the house when they bought it many years before and had not been looked into since. Remember that Pat was still working as a full-time teacher. She had to find a place to live, pack up her stuff, and move out of her family home in her time off. The clock was ticking. Rummaging through those boxes under the soot and ash, the stress of her moving schedule, resulted in Pat contracting pneumonia. At that point, she had to hire someone to simply move the attic boxes to her new apartment. The mover stacked those 50 boxes against the wall of her new garage.

The attic boxes sat quietly and undisturbed for a few years inside the garage at the new apartment. Finally, Pat's daughter offered to help her sort through them. She agreed and one day they got together to tackle it. Some of these boxes had not been unpacked since the 1970s. After a couple of hours, Pat dramatically pretended to swoon, grasp her chest, and fall on the floor. Her daughter, confused, rushed to her side and said, "Mom! Are you alright?" Pat responded, "I can't do this anymore. Pretend I died, and it's all yours." Pat's wonderful daughter agreed. Always organized and practical, her daughter was able to sell, donate, and throw away everything. She saved a few things that she knew Pat would want. One thing was a tiny sorority pin that Pat had not seen in decades. Otherwise, she was delighted to have all of that off her hands.

Pat's advice on downsizing: "Get a friend or family member to help you. And, if that stuff has sat there for a long time, and you're not doing anything with it now, you never will. Get rid of it."

PAT'S PLAN B

Now Pat is 77 years old. She has lived in the beautiful, sunny, centrally located apartment for over 15 years. Though Pat has had both knees replaced and suffered a heart attack last year, she is a very active senior. She plays tennis once a week, she goes to a kickboxing class at the gym, she regularly meets with friends and enjoys cultural activities in her city.

When asked about her Plan B, Pat is ready with an answer. She is fortunate that both her children have offered to have her live with them, but she adamantly declined. Instead, she prefers to plan for what her father did when he was aging in another state. She visited him at his retirement community and was impressed with what she saw. He had many activities to choose from, there were friendly staff and a social group of people to keep him company. With this positive example, Pat knew what she was looking for. A friend had expressed concern about what these places were like. Pat said to her "Well, why don't we go take a look?" So, Pat and her friend went to look at a number of local senior homes. They ranged from the three-tiered homes that include independent, assisted, and memory care; some were older and more established and some were recently built with added amenities. While her friend was still troubled by how many "old people in wheelchairs" were in some of the places they visited, Pat was more accepting of that. She has made a decision about which one suits her needs and preferences. She has discussed this with both of her children and the family is in agreement that when the time comes, that is where she will move to.

BEAUTIFUL SUMMERS – NOT JUST FOR THE RICH AND FAMOUS

We can't leave Pat's story until we share one of the most creative and enriching parts of her life. It is a great example of reaching for what you want at any age. It also conveys how a flexible mindset can open up possibilities.

As a school teacher, Pat had the summers off. Like most other teachers, it did not mean that she was unemployed. She needed year-round income to pay her bills. Many summers, she would work at summer camps.

She also loved to travel. She and some fellow teachers enjoyed traveling up and down the California coast during the shorter school spring break. When they got to Santa Barbara on one of their trips, Pat fell in love with the area. The next summer, Pat decided that she wanted to go back there, for the whole summer. Her daughters were near college age and had their dad's supervision. Pat got a job at a summer camp in Santa Barbara and rented a room in someone's house. In the middle of the summer, one of the camp teachers had to leave suddenly for a family emergency in another country. She asked if Pat would house sit while she was gone for a few weeks and take care of her cats.

This got Pat started. She used word of mouth and put an ad in the Santa Barbara classifieds. She became a summer housesitter, offering her services to care for all different kinds of pets. "Except for snakes, I don't do snakes." She has taken care of wild dogs that have tangled with skunks, super large aquariums and is thankful that she has only killed one houseplant.

This new role has allowed her to stay for free in one of her favorite cities in the world every summer. She does a minimum of 3 weeks and a maximum of 6 weeks to work with her school schedule. One family arranged with her to stay in their home every summer for 10 consecutive years. Early on, she continued to teach at summer sports camps and tennis at the county education facility. Later, she became active with a bike club and would do 25-mile rides with them before her knee problems. She takes art classes and has made many lifetime friends in the area. She loves the ocean and has a favorite beach that she goes to with friends for occasional picnics.

Pat continued her annual summer house sitting trips into retirement. Last summer was her 30th year. When we last spoke, it looked like coronavirus would interfere with her plan for this year. But, she has every intention to resume when the coast is clear.

WHAT HAPPENED TO PAT WHEN COVID HIT?

Pat has continued to do her weekly fitness classes as her gym switched to the virtual streaming format. She has multiple zoom meetings with friends and her book club. She has family nearby who assist her with grocery shopping. She was delighted that she would finally be getting her haircut after 3 months.

SOME FINAL THOUGHTS-KEEP AN OPEN MIND TO FIND THE PLACE THAT IS HOME

Throughout this book, we have approached the question of where to live as you age with a combination of creativity, a big dose of reality, and an open mind. Aging can be a wild card or a smooth sail into the sunset. Retirement for many must be postponed due to financial needs. And, very few want to sit on the porch in a rocking chair doing nothing.

A last thought as you continue the process of finding the right home for you as you age. Don't put off thinking about this. We get a little bit older every day. Denial of aging and its relentless approach can be a short term comfort but may result in fewer long term choices.

We have known many older people who refuse to believe that anything about their life will change. Suddenly, they find themselves unable to do things in the same way. They struggle and resist.

Most of the people and their stories that you have met in these pages have faced their futures head on. They have been realistic and thoughtful. Sometimes they have had to go back to the drawing board and revamp the plan. But, largely, they have continued to be the architect of their own home. And we wish that for all of us as we age.

NOTES

I. NECESSITY IS THE MOTHER OF INVENTION

1 "Cost of Care Survey," *Genworth*, accessed June 20, 2020.
2 Betty Friedan, *The Fountain of Age*, (Simon and Schuster, New York, New York, 1993), 510.
3 Marni Jameson, *Downsizing the Family Home: What to Save, What to Let Go*, AARP/Sterling, January 5, 2016.
4 Nadia Balint, "The Biggest Game Changers in Renting Are Older, Highly-Educated Renters, and 2.5 Million Stronger," *rentcafe.com*, October 17, 2017. https://www.rentcafe.com/blog/rental-market/real-estate-news/todayrenterprofile-older-highly-educated-suburban/
5 Richard Eisenberg, "The Distressing Growth of Wealth Inequality of Boomers," *Nextavenue.org*, October 16, 2019. Accessed June 20, 2020. https://www.nextavenue.org/wealth-inequality-of-boomers/

2. THE ALLURE OF COHOUSING

6 Cohousing An Association a Community of Communities. https://www.cohousing.org/directory
7 "Dynamic Governance," *Creative Learning Solutions Inc.com*, Accessed June 20, 2020. http://www.clsolutionsinc.com/what-we-do/dynamic-governance/

3. THE GOLDEN GIRLS INSPIRED HOUSE

8   Chase Banger, "Golden Girls for Real: Rockwood Retirees Looking for Roomies," *ctvnews.ca*, March 28, 2019 Accessed June 20,
2020.

9   "So What is a Homestay?" *Homestay.com*, October 1, 2017, Accessed
June 20, 2020. https://www.homestay.com/blog/2017/10/01/so-what-
is-a-homestay

10 Janelle Orsi, "Legal and Financial Issues to Consider When Co-
Owning a Home," *nolo.com*, Accessed June 20, 2020. https://www.
nolo.com/legal-encyclopedia/legal-financial-issues-consider-
when-co-owning-home.html

11 National Alliance for Caregiving, Public Policy Institute, "Caregiving in the United States 2020", accessed June 20, 2020.

12 "Cost of Care Survey," *Genworth*, accessed June 20, 2020. https://
www.genworth.com/aging-and-you/finances/cost-of-care.html

4. THE FAMILY TRADITION: MOVING
IN WITH THE KIDS

13 Patrick Kiger, "More Older Adults Are Moving in With Their
Children," *AARP*, February 5, 2018, accessed June 20, 2020.
https://www.aarp.org/home-family/friends-family/info-2018/
adults-live-with-children-fd.html

14 Stephanie Firestone, "Incentivizing Multigenerational Living,"
AARP, May 23, 2019. https://blog.aarp.org/thinking-policy/incentivizing-
multigenerational-living

15 D'Vera Cohn and Jeffrey S. Passal, "A Record 64 Million Americans
Live in Multi-Generational Households," *Pew Research Center*,
April 5, 2018, Accessed June 20, 2020. https://www.pewresearch.
org/fact-tank/2018/04/05/a-record-64-million-americans-live-in-
multigenerational-households/

16 National Alliance for Caregiving, Public Policy Institute, "Caregiving in the United States 2020", accessed June 20, 2020.

17 "Cost of Care Survey," *Genworth*, accessed June 20, 2020. https://
www.genworth.com/aging-and-you/finances/cost-of-care.html

5. NEW FRONTIERS IN SENIOR HOUSING

18 Abby Hayes, "What You Need to Know About the Holiday Inn Retirement Plan," *Dough Roller*, May 25, 2020, Accessed June 20, 2020. https://www.doughroller.net/retirement-planning/what-you-need-to-know-about-the-holiday-inn-retirement-plan/

19 Lana Bandoim, "Are Luxury Cruise Ships the Next Retirement Plan?" *The Week*, May 29, 2019, accessed June 20, 2020. https://theweek.com/articles/837253/are-luxury-cruise-ships-new-retirement-homes

20 Alanna Zingara, https://www.youtube.com/watch?v=6878WSc WG0Y

21 Mary Kate Nelson, "Co-Living Start-Up Ollie Draws Aging Baby Boomers," *Senior Housing News*, November 27, 2017, accessed June 20, 2020. https://seniorhousingnews.com/2017/11/27/co-living-startup-ollie-draws-aging-baby-boomers/

22 "Tiny House Movement," Wikipedia, accessed June 24, 2020. https://en.wikipedia.org/wiki/Tiny_house_movement#cite_note-1

23 "Tiny House Designed to be Elderly/Disability/Mobility Friendly" *Living Big in a Tiny House*, January 4, 2019, accessed June 20, 2020. https://www.youtube.com/watch?v=BlQ3yuUmBiw&feature=share

24 Annie Clark and Cory Smith, "Life on a College or University Campus-An Alternative Retirement Destination," *The Senior List*, September 24, 2019, accessed June 20, 2020. https://www.theseniorlist.com/retirement/best/university/

25 Jon Marcus, "New College Communities Custom-Built for Retirees," *AARP*, August 14, 2019, accessed June 20, 2020. https://www.aarp.org/retirement/planning-for-retirement/info-2019/colleges-with-retirement-communities.html

26 Chuck Sudo, "Clean Slate Project Offers Blueprint for Senior Living's Future," *Senior Housing News*, June 6, 2019. Accessed June 5, 2020. https://seniorhousingnews.com/2019/06/06/clean-slate-project-offers-blueprint-for-senior-livings-future/

6. BECOMING THE EXPAT

27 Doug Walker, "Social Security Benefits U.S. Citizens Outside the United States," socialsecurity.gov, August 8, 2016, accessed June 20, 2020. https://blog.ssa.gov/social-security-benefits-u-s-citizens-outside-the-united-states/

28 Travel.State. Gov.https://travel.state.gov/content/travel/en/international-travel.html

29 Rebecca Lake, "Best Countries for Retirement Abroad," *Investopedia*, August 21, 2019, accessed June 20, 2020. https://www.investopedia.com/retirement/best-countries-to-retire/

30 Travel.State. Gov.https://travel.state.gov/content/travel/en/us-visas/visa-information-resources/list-of-posts.html

31 William P. Barrett, "The Best Places to Retire Abroad in 2019," *Forbes*, November 19, 2018, accessed June 20, 2020. https://www.forbes.com/sites/williampbarrett/2018/11/19/best-places-retire-abroad/#17bf0ed43214

7. WHAT IF IT DOESN'T WORK OUT? PLAN B AND C

32 Jules Rosen MD, "A Doctor's View: Depression in Long-Term Care Residents." *Journal of the Catholic Health Association of the United States*, November-December 2014, accessed June 20, 2020. https://www.chausa.org/publications/health-progress/article/november-december-2014/a-doctor%27s-view-depression-in-long-term-care-residents

33 Kate Jackson, "Prevent Elder Transfer Trauma: Tips to Ease Relocation Stress." *Social Work Today*, January/February 2015, accessed June 5, 2020. https://www.socialworktoday.com/archive/011915p10.shtml

8. SUPER AGERS ROLL WITH THE PUNCHES

34 Flexibility,https://en.wikipedia.org/wiki/Flexibility_(personality)

BIBLIOGRAPHY

Balint, Nadia. "The Biggest Game Changers in Renting Are Older, Highly-Educated Renters, and 2.5 Million Stronger." rentcafe.com. October 17, 2017. Accessed June 20, 2020. https://www.rentcafe.com/blog/rental-market/real-estate-news/todayrenterprofile-older-highly-educated-suburban/

Bandoim, Lana. "Are Luxury Cruise Ships the Next Retirement Plan?" *The Week*. May 29, 2019. Accessed June 20, 2020. https://theweek.com/articles/837253/are-luxury-cruise-ships-new-retirement-homes

Banger, Chase. "Golden Girls for Real: Rockwood Retirees Looking for Roomies." ctvnews.ca. March 28, 2019. Accessed June 20, 2020. https://kitchener.ctvnews.ca/golden-girls-for-real-rockwood-retiree-looking-for-roomies-1.4356199

Barrett, William P. The Best Places to Retire Abroad in 2019. https://www.forbes.com/sites/williampbarrett/2018/11/19/best-places-retire-abroad/#17bf0ed43214

Cohn, D'Vera and Jeffrey S. Passal. "A Record 64 Million Americans Live in Multi-Generational Households." *Pew Research Center*. April 5, 2018. Accessed June 20, 2020. https://www.pewresearch.org/fact-tank/2018/04/05/a-record-64-million-americans-live-in-multigenerational-households/

Clark, Annie, and Cory Smith. "Life on a College or University Campus-An Alternative Retirement Destination." *The Senior*

List. September 24, 2019. Accessed June 20, 2020. https://www. theseniorlist.com/retirement/best/university/

Creative Learning Solutions Inc.com. "Cohousing An Association a Community of Communities." Accessed June 20, 2020. https:// www.cohousing.org/directory

Creative Learning Solutions Inc.com. "Dynamic Governance." Accessed June 20, 2020. http://www.clsolutionsinc.com/what-we-do/ dynamic-governance/

Eisenberg, Richard. "The Distressing Growth of Wealth Inequality of Boomers" *Next Avenue.* October 16, 2019. Accessed June 20, 2020. https://www.nextavenue.org/wealth-inequality-of-boomers/

Firestone, Stephanie. "Incentivizing Multigenerational Living." *AARP.* May 23, 2019. Accessed June 20, 2020. https://blog.aarp. org/thinking-policy/incentivizing-multigenerational-living

Friedan, Betty. *The Fountain of Age.* Simon and Schuster. New York, New York. 1993.

Genworth. "Cost of Care Survey." *Genworth.* Accessed June 20, 2020. https://www.genworth.com/aging-and-you/finances/cost-of-care. html

Hayes, Abby. "What You Need to Know About the Holiday Inn Retirement Plan." *DoughRoller.* May 25, 2020. Accessed June 20, 2020. https://www.doughroller.net/retirement-planning/what-you-need-to-know-about-the-holiday-inn-retirement-plan/

Homestay.com. "So What is a Homestay?" October 1, 2017, Accessed June 20, 2020. https://www.homestay.com/blog/2017/10/01/so-what-is-a-homestay

Jackson, Kate. "Prevent Elder Transfer Trauma: Tips to Ease Relocation Stress." *Social Work Today.* January/February 2015. Accessed June 5, 2020. https://www.socialworktoday.com/archive/011915p10.shtml

Jameson, Marni. *Downsizing the Family Home: What to Save, What to Let Go.* AARP/Sterling. 2016.

Kiger, Patrick. "More Older Adults Are Moving in With Their Children." *AARP.* February 5, 2018. Accessed June 20, 2020. https://www. aarp.org/home-family/friends-family/info-2018/adults-live-with-children-fd.html

Lake, Rebecca. Best Countries for Retirement Abroad. https://www. investopedia.com/retirement/best-countries-to-retire/

Marcus, Jon. "New College Communities Custom-Built for Retirees." *AARP*. August 14, 2019. Accessed June 20, 2020. https://www. aarp.org/retirement/planning-for-retirement/info-2019/colleges-with-retirement-communities.html

National Alliance for Caregiving. Public Policy Institute. "Caregiving in the United States 2020." Accessed June 20, 2020. https://www. caregiving.org/caregiving-in-the-us-2020/

Nelson, Mary Kate. "Co-Living Start-Up Ollie Draws Aging Baby Boomers." *Senior Housing News*. November 27, 2017. Accessed June 20, 2020. https://seniorhousingnews.com/2017/11/27/co-living-startup-ollie-draws-aging-baby-boomers/

Orsi, Janelle. "Legal and Financial Issues to Consider When Co-Owning a Home." nolo.com. Accessed June 20, 2020. https://www. nolo.com/legal-encyclopedia/legal-financial-issues-consider-when-co-owning-home.html

Pender, Kathleen. "Senior Cohousing an Antidote to Loneliness that Hits People As They Age." *San Francisco Chronicle*. January 5, 2019. Accessed June 20, 2020. https://www.sfchronicle.com/business/ networth/article/Senior-cohousing-an-antidote-to-the-13510258. php?cmp=EMC-DSM – NLC-LC-HOMFAM-20190206_Li vableCommunities_700500_1032702-020619-F5-Cohousing-Text-CTRL-3554043&mi_u=34659623&mi_ecmp=20190206_ LivableCommunities_700500_1032702&encparam=5twEhAd HiD4THDbr88CIEjxKhKi%2BqKHdyr7RsoJnye4%3D&fbc lid=IwAR19jHPmH6eGt3FIZthCIxsbBBPbCGcVjnNsqnz6r CJN-w3fRfwtlkgP97A&psid=5fQBg

Rosen, Jules MD. "A Doctor's View: Depression in Long-Term Care Residents." *Journal of the Catholic Health Association of the United States*. November-December 2014. Accessed June 20, 2020. https://www.chausa.org/publications/health-progress/article/ november-december-2014/a-doctor%27s-view-depression-in-long-term-care-residents

Sudo, Chuck. "Clean Slate Project Offers Blueprint for Senior Living's Future." *Senior Housing News*. June 6, 2019. Accessed June 5, 2020. https://seniorhousingnews.com/2019/06/06/clean-slate-project-offers-blueprint-for-senior-livings-future/

"Tiny House Designed to be Elderly/Disability/Mobility Friendly."

Living Big in a Tiny House. January 4, 2019. Accessed June 20, 2020. https://www.youtube.com/watch?v=BlQ3yuUmBiw&feature=share

"Tiny House Movement." Wikipedia. Accessed June 24, 2020. https://en.wikipedia.org/wiki/Tiny_house_movement#cite_note-1

Travel.State.Gov.https://travel.state.gov/content/travel/en/international-travel.html

Travel.State.Gov.   https://travel.state.gov/content/travel/en/us-visas/visa-information-resources/list-of-posts.html

Walker, Doug. Social Security Benefits U.S. Citizens Outside the United States. https://blog.ssa.gov/social-security-benefits-u-s-citizens-outside-the-united-states/. Accessed September 30, 2020.

Wikipedia. "Flexibility (Personality)." *Wikipedia.* Accessed June 5, 2020. https://en.wikipedia.org/wiki/Flexibility_(personality)

Verde, Tom. "There's Community and Consensus. But No Commune." *The New York Times.* January 20, 2018. Accessed June 20, 2020. https://www.nytimes.com/2018/01/20/business/cohousing-communities.html?fbclid=IwAR0fGa11fjva0QHfMRhARBWD_DlJ3E-s9ex1cHEJdsduNtf6NhaUp2ra0pM

Zingano, Alanna. "Where are They Now? Living At Sea Full-Time Cruisers During Pandemic." April 27, 2020. https://www.youtube.com/watch?v=6878WScWG0Y. Accessed September 30, 2020.

INDEX

CPSIA information can be obtained
at www.ICGtesting.com
Printed in the USA
LVHW030159050121
675394LV00006B/513